VERY GOOD

God's Plan for You, in You, and through You

Jim Nave

ISBN 979-8-89043-216-2 (paperback)
ISBN 979-8-89043-217-9 (digital)

Christian Faith Publishing
832 Park Avenue
Meadville, PA 16335
www.christianfaithpublishing.com

Printed in the United States of America

DEDICATION

I WOULD LIKE to dedicate this book first and foremost to Teresa: my wife, friend, soul mate, lover and ministry partner. Without your encouragement, support, trust, patience and editorial skills this book would never have come to fruition.

To my children: Joshua, Ashley, Chelsea, Jordan and Jacob; your encouragement and support were instrumental in its completion.

To my grandchildren: you were the inspiration for me to write this book. I want you to know the truth about the goodness of God and his amazing plan for your lives.

I would also like to thank the pastors and church families that have poured into my life over the last three decades. You all have been such a blessing to me, and I will forever be grateful.

PREFACE

A Very Good God with Very Good Plans for You

The book of Genesis is the book of beginnings. It is how everything began. Do you realize there was a prequel to Genesis? Do you really think that George Lucas came up with the idea of a prequel to continue the global success of *Star Wars*? No! It was God's idea.

"In Christ, he chose us before the world was made. He chose us in love to be his holy people—people who could stand before him without any fault" (Ephesians 1:4 ERV).

All of God's plans began with us in mind! We are the apple of God's eye, the crown jewel of creation, the object of his affection.

Before God created the earth, he anticipated every want, need, and desire that we would ever have, and it was all based on his nature. God is the source of everything that you need. His plan is that we would live in a relationship with him based on dependency and trust in him as our source.

Before God even created Adam and Eve, he put everything we need in and on the earth. Then, after our needs were met, he created man in his image and likeness.

"Then God said, 'Let Us make man in *Our image* [emphasis mine] according to *Our likeness* [emphasis mine]; let them have dominion over the fish of the sea, over the birds of the air, and over the cattle, over all the earth and over every creeping thing that creeps on the earth'" (Genesis 1:26).

- Image is our capacity to receive the nature of God.
- Likeness is our capacity to reveal the nature of God

As the crown jewel of God's creation, we are the only created beings with the capacity to receive and reveal the nature of God, which is our divine purpose. You and I were created to reveal the nature of God to the world.

God established himself as the source of life and created the perfect habitation for us. Then he created us in his image and likeness with the divine purpose of living in a relationship with him, based on dependency and trust with the purpose of revealing his glory to the world. When all of this was finished, he said it was *very good*!

God has a very good plan for your life.

"'I say this because I know the plans that I have for you.' This message is from the Lord. 'I have *good* [emphasis mine] plans for you. I don't plan to hurt you. I plan to give you hope and a *good future* [emphasis mine]'" (Jeremiah 29:11 ERV).

To live out the very good life that God has for you, you have to discover four things:

1) The true nature of God.

The only way to discover the true nature of God is to see it lived out in the life of Jesus.

"He (Jesus) is the radiance of the glory of God and the exact imprint of his nature" (Hebrews 1:3a ESV).

2) How God *has already* fulfilled his redemptive plans for us through Jesus.

"For all of God's promises have been fulfilled in Christ with a resounding 'Yes!' And through Christ, our 'Amen' (which means 'Yes') ascends to God for his glory" (2 Corinthians 1:20 NLT).

3) What God's redemptive plans are for us.

"For God knew his people in advance, and he chose them to become like his Son, so that his Son would be the firstborn among many brothers and sisters" (Romans 8:29 NLT).

4) How he intended for us to receive what he has already provided.

"Now faith is the assurance (title deed, confirmation) of things hoped for (divinely guaranteed), and the evidence of things not seen [the conviction of their reality—faith comprehends as fact what cannot be experienced by the physical senses]" (Hebrews 11:1 AMP).

In this book, God will reveal to you the truth about who he says you are because of what Jesus has already done. You will learn how to develop and use your faith based on how he created you so that you can receive and experience the very good plan that God has for your life.

INTRODUCTION

The Truth That Sets You Free

Jesus gives us a very clear definition of why he came. John 10:10b says, "I have come that they may have life, and that they may have it more abundantly."

According to the *Strong's Concordance*, the word *abundant* means "super abundance, excessive, overflowing, over and above, extraordinary, more than sufficient, enough, and extra." This describes God's design for us or what life was like before sin entered into the human experience because of the disobedience of Adam.

Jesus came to restore this life for us through his death, burial, and resurrection. The finished work of Jesus *has* set us free from the nature, power, and effects of sin, the power and influence of Satan, and even the power of death itself. Knowing this truth is what will set you free!

In the first half of verse 10, Jesus tells us Satan's plan. John 10:10a says, "The thief does not come except to steal, and to kill, and to destroy." The word *destroy* means "to annihilate a thing or a form in which it exists."

Jesus has already paid the price to set you free from all of the effects of the fall and restore the abundant life that God created for us. Satan is trying to destroy Jesus's work through his power of deception.

Deception means "to believe what is false or disbelieve what is true."

Satan began his deceptive tactics in the garden by calling into question the nature and plan of God. Did God really say? Satan never tries to totally change the truth of the Gospel. He simply twists and tweaks it until we are led to believe in a gospel that is void of the power to set us free from sin, Satan, and death.

Let me illustrate these deceptions for you.

Many of us have been taught that eternal life is describing a future hope of heaven. "For God so loved the world that he gave his one and only Son, that whoever believes in him shall not perish but have eternal life" (John 3:16 NIV).

So what about today? Did Jesus pay the ultimate price of his life for a future hope and leave us bound by the effects of sin and Satan today? Jesus never intended for you to wait until you die to experience the benefits of his salvation. The apostle Paul said, "Who gave Himself for our sins, that He might deliver us from this *present evil age* [emphasis mine], according to the will of our God and Father" (Galatians 1:4).

The truth about salvation

Salvation is the biblical word that describes the redemptive work of Jesus through his death, burial, and resurrection. For us to experience the benefits of salvation, we need to know the truth of what is included.

In Romans 10:9–10 (NKJV), Paul describes how we receive salvation. "That if thou shalt confess with thy mouth the Lord Jesus, and shalt believe in thine heart that God hath raised him from the dead, thou shalt be *saved* [emphasis mine]. For with the heart man believeth unto righteousness; and with the mouth confession is made unto *salvation* [emphasis mine]."

Believe with your heart and confess with your mouth, but he also uses both words that describe this great gift of redemption—*save* and *salvation.*

If you go to any Greek concordance written by any scholar, no matter what denomination he is associated with, it will always say the same thing. The word for save is *sozo*. It means to be healed, delivered, restored, protected, made whole. The word for salvation is *soteria*. It, too, means to be healed, delivered, restored, protected, and made whole.

Like most of you, I always thought that being saved meant being forgiven of my sin so that I could go to heaven. Well, that is true, just not the whole truth. You can be forgiven of your sin yet still live under the power and effects of sin and Satan. That is not the abundant life that Jesus paid for.

Understanding the power of the finished work of Christ

"For the grace of God that brings salvation *has* [emphasis mine] appeared to all men" (Titus 2:11 NKJV).

Do you see that salvation is being presented as a past tense accomplishment? Jesus paid for our salvation two thousand years ago through his death, burial, and resurrection.

Now let's go back and insert these other benefits of salvation into this verse so that we can begin to get a revelation of how the Bible describes salvation.

- The grace of God that *restores* relationship with God *has* appeared to all men.
- The grace of God that brings *healing* and *wholeness has* appeared to all men.
- The grace of God that brings *deliverance* from the power of sin, Satan, and death *has* appeared unto all men.

Let's continue to look at how the finished work of Christ is presented in the Epistles.

"Everything we could ever need for life and godliness *has* [emphasis mine] already been deposited in us by his divine power" (2 Peter 1:1 TPT).

"For He *has* [emphasis mine] rescued us and *has* [emphasis mine] drawn us to Himself from the dominion of darkness, and *has* [emphasis mine] transferred us to the kingdom of His beloved Son" (Colossians 1:13 AMP).

"Blessed be the God and Father of our Lord Jesus Christ, who *has* [emphasis mine] blessed us with every spiritual blessing in the heavenly places in Christ" (Ephesians 1:3 NKJV).

"Who Himself bore our sins in His own body on the tree, that we, having died to sins, might live for righteousness—by whose stripes you *were* [emphasis mine] healed" (1 Peter 2:24 NKJV).

Do you see it? Every one of these verses that describe the redemptive work of Jesus presents them as a past tense accomplishment. Why? Because Jesus died, was buried, and resurrected only one time, and that was enough to remove all the effects of sin, conquer Satan and death, and provide an abundant life to everyone who will believe and receive this great gift.

A beautiful prophetic picture

In the six days of creation, God created the perfect environment that would provide for all the wants, needs, and desires of its inhabitants. Then he made man his perfect image bearers, and he gave them stewardship over his creation. On the seventh day, he rested. Was he exhausted from creation? Would he pass out and die if he created one more rose? No, he rested because his part was done, and all his people had to do was receive this abundant life as a gift and enjoy it.

Now let's take a look at Jesus. Hebrews 10:12 says, "But this Man, after He had offered one sacrifice for sins forever, sat down at the right hand of God." After he provided a one-time sacrifice that would set us free from the power and effects of sin, Satan, and death and restore the abundant life we were created for, he sat down at the right hand of the Father. Why? Was he exhausted? *No*! His part was finished, and now all we have to do is receive this abundant life as a gift and enjoy it.

Here is the deception: many of us have been taught that only the forgiveness of sin was paid for through the atonement. All the other benefits of salvation—healing, deliverance, and restoration—are present/future tense possibilities based on the mysterious will of God and were not provided for in the atonement.

Satan knows a lot about faith. He knows that we can't believe (be fully persuaded) about something that hasn't already been accomplished, and he knows that you can't receive what you don't believe.

Satan doesn't care if you believe that God can do anything as long as you believe that there are certain things he has not already done.

We are praying to Jesus to intercede for us and convince God to *do something* on our behalf. Jesus is interceding with God that we would believe and receive what he has already *done*.

The apostle Paul had the great privilege to pray for the church of Jesus Christ, which includes us. These prayers are found in both the books of Ephesians and Colossians. You can tell a lot about what people believe based on how they pray. Paul was fully convinced about the finished work of Jesus, the great gift of salvation that was already paid for, so he never prayed for a new move of God, a special healing anointing, a greater power of deliverance, or a double portion. He prayed that we would get a greater revelation of what *Jesus had already provided*!

"I pray that the light of God will illuminate the eyes of your imagination, flooding you with light, until you experience the full revelation of the hope of his calling —that is, the wealth of God's glorious inheritances that he finds in us, his holy ones!" (Ephesians 1:18 TPT).

Your inheritance is that through Jesus, you *have been* restored back into a relationship with the source of life and restored into the image and likeness of God so that you can fulfill your purpose of revealing his nature to a lost and dying world.

I can hear your question, "If that is true, why am I not experiencing these amazing promises?" Remember the old Wendy's commercial, "Where's the beef?"

The key to receiving all of the promises that Jesus has already paid for is to understand how to function in both the natural (seen) and spiritual (unseen) realms.

Let me illustrate.

- Natural realm—what you see, hear, taste, smell, or touch.

Right now you are in a physical room, sitting in a physical chair, reading a physical book. At the same time, there are millions of data points being sent from computer to computer; there are movies, sporting events, and music that are being streamed all around you yet you cannot see them. All of this invisible information is just as real as the chair you are sitting on, even though you cannot see it with your natural eyes.

So how do you enjoy the benefits of what is already available in the invisible? You need something that can receive and reveal (transmit) the signals.

All of your electronics, whether it is your TV, smartphone, or your tablet, were all designed to receive these invisible signals, convert them, then transmit, or reveal them to you in the seen realm.

- Spiritual realm.

God is a Spirit. He lives and functions in the spiritual or invisible realm. John 6:63 (NKJV) reveals this truth to us, "It is the Spirit who gives life; the flesh profits nothing. The words that I speak to you are spirit, and they are life." Jesus is telling us that his Word is Spirit, which means that it is revealing spiritual (unseen), not natural (seen) realities.

Every redemptive promise has already been paid for, and it already exists in the unseen realm of the spirit. These promises are just as real as the fact that right now there is a signal broadcasting reruns of *CSI: New York*.

What you need is something that can receive these unseen realities and transmit or reveal them in the seen realm. Here is the best news ever. This is why you were created. You were created to receive and reveal the nature of this amazing unseen God. Your spirit is your receiver. In your spirit, all of the promises already exist, and God has given you a way to reveal these spiritual realities into the natural, through your transmitter called faith. "Now faith is the assurance (title deed, confirmation) of things hoped for (divinely guaranteed), and the evidence of things not seen [the conviction of their reality—faith comprehends as fact what cannot be experienced by the physical senses]" (Hebrews 11:1 AMP).

Do you see what God has been trying to reveal to us all along? When you get born again, you are given everything you need for life and godliness, every benefit of salvation, healing, deliverance, restoration, protection, and wholeness. It is already in you in the unseen realm of your spirit. God gave you a gift called faith so that you can believe and receive what he has already provided based on the truth of God's Word.

With our natural mind, we only believe what we can see, taste, hear, smell, and feel. In our spirit, by faith, we can believe what we cannot see based on the truths of God's promises. "Jesus said to him, 'If you can believe, *all things are possible to him who believes* [emphasis mine]'" (Mark 9:23 NKJV).

CHAPTER 1

Knowing God

God is love!

"GOD IS LOVE, and anyone who doesn't love others has never known him" (1 John 4:8 CEV).

What you believe about yourself begins and ends with what you believe about God.

Genesis 1:27 says that you were "made in the image of God." What does that mean? What is he truly like? Does he even exist? Is he good, bad, or indifferent? Is he a loving Father that always wants what's best for me? Quick to forgive and always merciful? Or is he a righteous judge who loves me based solely on my behavior? Is he like an overbearing father that you just can't quite please, no matter how hard you try?

The most important thing we all must know is the true nature of God! He has many attributes but one essence. Essence: that which makes something what it is; intrinsic, fundamental nature, or most important quality (of something); essential being (yourdictionary.com). Essence is the fundamental nature or the motivating force behind everything one does.

God is multifaceted. He is gracious, just, kind, holy, righteous, all-knowing, all-powerful. The list goes on and on, but what is his essence?

A few years ago, I taught a series called "Trustworthy" about the names of God. As I was studying the name Elohim (the strong Creator God), I just took some time to meditate on the name and ask for revelation to help me better understand. I heard a voice, not an audible voice but an inner witness say, "All of my plans flow from my nature, and all of my promises are backed by my nature." I knew immediately it was a true revelation from God that would change the way I viewed him and, therefore, how I viewed myself. This has also become the lens that has reshaped my theology. I realized that I had to take all of my theological positions and run them through the lens of God's nature. If they disagree with God's nature, they had to be disregarded, no matter how passionate I was about it because God's nature is unchanging.

Because all of God's plans flow from his nature, then it is imperative that we know his true essence. Remember, essence is the motivating force behind everything that one does. So let's look at what God did and see what's behind everything he does.

One of the most well-known Bible verses worldwide is John 3:16, and it says, "For God so loved the world that he gave his one and only Son, that whoever believes in him shall not perish but have eternal life." It is clear from this verse alone that love motivated God to send Jesus to restore what was lost in the fall.

When the apostle John (the one whom Jesus loved) described the essence of God, he said, "God is love" (1 John 4:8 CEV).

When Jesus described the two greatest commandments that would reflect the Father's heart, he said, "Love the Lord your God with all your heart and with all your soul and with all your mind. This is the first and greatest commandment. And the second is like it: Love your neighbor as yourself" (Matthew 22:37–39 NIV).

When Jesus described how people would know that we are God's image bearers, he said, "A new command I give you: Love one another. As I have loved you, so you must love one another. By this everyone will know that you are my disciples, if you love one another" (John 13:34–35).

I have come to a deep conviction that the true essence of God's nature is love! This truth has changed the way I view God, myself, and others. As I began to see God's plans through the lens of his love, my theology began to take on a new meaning.

Now that we understand the essence of God's nature and the truth that all of God's plans flow from his nature, let's look at how our story began. "Then God said, 'Let us make a man—someone like ourselves, to be the master of all life upon the earth and in the skies and in the seas'" (Genesis 1:26 Living Bible).

God's love is the reason he created mankind. Did he create man because he was in need of love and needed people to love, honor, and adore him? No, quite the opposite. He created man because love has to be expressed. Love only works within the context of relationship. *God made man as the object of his affection.*

Here's how it all began. Before the foundation of the world, God dreamed of a family. His desire was for man to be blessed (divine empowerment to increase and prosper). "Blessed be the God and Father of our Lord Jesus Christ, who has *blessed* [emphasis mine] us with every spiritual blessing in the heavenly places in Christ, just as He chose us in Him before the foundation of the world, that we should be holy and without blame before Him in love, having predestined us to *adoption as sons* [emphasis mine] by Jesus Christ to Himself, according to the good pleasure of His will" (Ephesians 1:3–5 NKJV).

Because God is love, he anticipated every need man would ever have, and he created a perfect environment for him to ensure that his promise of abundance and blessing can always be experienced. All of this was done before he created the first man.

Before Adam was formed from the dust of the ground, his four basic physical needs were already met.

1. God didn't wait for Adam to gasp for air and say, "I should have created oxygen."
2. God didn't wait for Adam to become thirsty and say, "I should have created water."
3. God didn't wait for Adam to experience hunger and say, "I should have created food."
4. God didn't wait for Adam to become exhausted and say, "I should have made a way for you to rest."

God is so loving that he made enough resources to meet not just Adam and Eve's needs but also the needs of all mankind.

1. We are still breathing from the same source of air today.
2. We are still drinking from the same source of water today.
3. We are still eating from the same source of food today.
4. We are still using the same source of rest today.

Think about this. God made food sources that would multiply after their own kind. The fruit you ate this week is part of God's original source. If you are a meat eater, your latest rib-eye steak came from that original source in the garden.

Not only did God anticipate and meet our basic physical needs—air, water, food, and rest before he created man—he also anticipated everything we would need to live an abundant life. Every article of clothing that would ever be worn, along with all of the accessories, hats, gloves, shoes, scarfs, every ring, necklace, and brooch. He anticipated every road, bridge, building, house, computer, car, truck, motorcycle, plane, train, and boat. Every kind of raw material that was needed to create all of these blessings was placed in and on the earth before a single person was made.

The same source of wood that built Noah's ark is still being used to build houses today. The same source of gold that was used to build Solomon's temple is being sold in retail stores all around the world today. Every farmer and rancher that has ever existed has been feeding their family and profiting from the same source that started in the garden.

And yet God wasn't done.

He anticipated every relationship; the intimacy between him and his children, the intimacy between husband and wife, parents and children, the deep bond that would be formed through close friendships. He anticipated every social activity: every friendship, date, wedding, worship service, and party. He is the source of all the relational tools we will ever need for these relationships to thrive and prosper.

After God had anticipated every need that man had, then he made man in his image and likeness.

- His image describes our identity (receiving God's nature).
- His likeness describes our purpose (revealing God's nature).

Let's let God describe himself to us

I am the source of light. Light always represents goodness; darkness always represent evil. "This is the message which we have heard from Him and declare to you, that God is light and in Him is no darkness at all" (1 John 1:5).

I am the source of all things. Source means first cause, origin, or that which something comes forth from. "Yet for us there is [only] one God, the Father, Who is the Source of all things and for Whom we [have life], and one Lord, Jesus Christ, through and by Whom are all things and through and by Whom we [ourselves exist]" (1 Corinthians 8:6 AMPC).

God's nature reveals that he is fully equipped to be the perfect source.

- He is omniscient: all-knowing, always aware of our every need.
- He is omnipresent: all-present, always within the midst of every need.
- He is omnipotent: all-powerful, always capable of meeting our every need.

God uses I Am statements to describe what his abundant provision is like.

I am Jehovah (the unchanging, eternal, self-existent God, the covenant-keeping God).

Then he began to reveal himself through a series of names. Every one reveals a different attribute of God's nature.

- I am *Jehovah Shammah*: the unchanging covenant-keeping God who is always with you.

Deuteronomy 31:8 states, "And the Lord, He is the One who goes before you. He will be with you, He will not leave you nor forsake you; do not fear nor be dismayed."

- I am *Jehovah Rohi*: the unchanging, covenant-keeping Shepherd. God is the source of spiritual leadership and wisdom. He leads and guides us.

Psalm 23:2 says, "He makes me to lie down in green pastures; He leads me beside the still waters."

- I am *Jehovah Jireh*: the unchanging, covenant-keeping source of provision.

Acts 17:25b states, "Since He gives to all life, breath, and all things."

- I am *Jehovah Shalom*: the unchanging, covenant-keeping source of peace.

Second Peter 1:2 (AMPC) says, "May grace (God's favor) and peace (which is perfect well-being, all necessary good, all spiritual prosperity, and freedom from fears and agitating passions and moral conflicts) be multiplied to you in [the full, personal, precise, and correct] knowledge of God and of Jesus our Lord."

- I am *Jehovah Nissi*: the unchanging, covenant-keeping source of victory.

First Corinthians 15:57 states, "But thanks be to God, who gives us the victory through our Lord Jesus Christ."

- I am *Jehovah Tsidkenu*: the unchanging, covenant-keeping source of righteousness.

Ephesians 4:24 says, "And that you put on the new man which was created according to God, in true righteousness and holiness."

- I am *Jehovah Rapha*: the unchanging, covenant-keeping source of divine health.

Exodus 15:26 states, "I am the Lord who heals you."

Because the essence of God is love, everything he does flows through the context of relationship. How did God design his family to live in a relationship with him as our source?

One day, I was in my office, meditating on these truths, and I saw a picture of Adam in my mind. Out of his lower back, he had this giant hose or line about two feet in diameter. At the end of this line, it had a fitting that could only connect to God as his source; this was his supply line. Then he had a small hose/line coming out of his chest, about six inches in diameter, with no fitting, and I realized that this was his outlet line.

The inlet line is how he stayed connected to or received the source of life. The outlet line is how he took what he received from God and revealed it to the people around him. This is a picture of image (inlet line) and likeness (outlet line).

God made his family with needs that only he could meet so that we would live in a relationship with him based on dependency and trust.

CHAPTER 2

Love Lost

So far, we've looked at the true meaning of salvation, the power of the finished work of Christ, God's invisible kingdom, and knowing God. All of these things reveal the goodness of God.

So what the heck happened in the garden?

In the garden, there were two trees. One was the tree of life. It represented the abundant life that was available as long as Adam and Eve stayed connected to the source of life. The other was the tree of the knowledge of good and evil and represented independence from God, self-effort, being the master of your own destiny, a God unto yourself.

Why two trees?

I have heard many people say that if God really loved us, he would not have given us a choice, and nobody would ever have been separated from him. The truth is love demands a choice. God did not want slaves. He wanted a family who would live in a relationship with him based on dependency and trust, and they would do it by choice.

I met my wife when she was nineteen. She was and still is beautiful, smart, caring, and compassionate. I knew after our first meeting that this was the kind of woman I wanted to spend the rest of my life with. The way I see it, I had two choices:

1) I could kidnap her and hope that it would break her will, and she would resign herself to living the rest of her life with me, but that's not love. That's slavery.

2) I could share my feelings with her and my desire to get to know her and invite her into a relationship based on choice.

She chose well, and we have been together over forty years. We have continued to develop an amazing relationship based on dependency and trust, just like the Father desires to have with us.

Back to the garden.

> Now the serpent was more crafty than any of the wild animals the Lord God had made. He said to the woman, "Did God really say, 'You must not eat from any tree in the garden?'" The woman said to the serpent, "We may eat fruit from the trees in the garden, but God did say, 'You must not eat fruit from the tree that is in the middle of the garden, and you must not touch it, or you will die.'" "You will not certainly die," the serpent said to the woman. "For God knows that when you eat from it your eyes will be opened, and you will be like God, knowing good and evil." (Genesis 3:1–5 NIV)

The enemy starts the conversation with Eve by asking, "Did God really say?" causing her to question the Word of God. His deception continues, "You will certainly not die," causing her to question the character of God. Then in his final act of deception, he convinced her that she did not need God, that if she ate the fruit, she would be a god, just like him. The truth was she was already made in his image and likeness.

The devastating results of the fall

To understand the effects of the fall on humanity, we need to know the root of sin is separation from the source of life. The behavior of sin is the fruit of that separation.

When Adam sinned, his supply line was severed, and he was separated from the source of abundance and lost all of the benefits that came from the source of life.

- Light: If you are separated from the source of light, what do you have? Darkness. Darkness represents living under the power and influence of a new source, Satan.
- Life: If you are separated from the source of life, what do you have? Death. Death robs our ability to both receive and produce the benefits of God's abundant design.
- Spiritual knowledge: If you are separated from the source of spiritual knowledge, what do you have? Ignorance or lack of knowledge. Ignorance robs us and keeps us in spiritual bondage because only knowledge of the truth can set you free.
- Provision: If you are separated from the source of provision, what do you have? Lack. Lack robs us from experiencing God's best and robs us of our ability to receive from God.
- Peace: If you are separated from the source of peace, what do you have? Stress. Stress robs your body of the ability to live a productive life.
- Victory: If you are separated from the source of victory, what do you have? Defeat. Defeat robs you of victory and the courage to fight the next fight.
- Righteousness: If you are separated from the source of righteousness, what do you have? Rejection. Rejection makes you feel unworthy and robs you of the confidence to come to God.
- Divine health: If you are separated from the source of divine health, what do you have? Sickness/disease. Sickness/disease robs you of the productivity and resources needed to fulfill your divine purpose.

Through the fall (separation from God), Satan was able to pervert God's design, and destruction was ushered in.

- Love became self-centeredness. Self-centeredness is the root cause of most of the tragedy on the planet. It happens when one person or group of people put their needs and desires above the value or dignity of others.
- Joy became despair. Despair causes insomnia, headaches, fatigue, chronic pain, increased risk of heart disease, inflammation, loss of libido, and poor digestive health.
- Peace became stress. Stress causes aches and pains, chest pain, or a feeling like your heart is racing, exhaustion or trouble sleeping, headaches, dizziness or shaking, high blood pressure, muscle tension, stomach or digestive problems, and if that wasn't bad enough, sexual dysfunction.
- Patience became intolerance.
- Goodness became wickedness.
- Kindness became hostility.
- Gentleness became harshness.
- Faithfulness became disloyalty.
- Self-control became self-indulgence.
- Provision became lack.
- Health became sickness.
- Life became death.

The perfect seed that was given to Adam to reproduce a perfect well-being was perverted, and sickness, disease, infirmity, and deformity began to be multiplied through mankind, contrary to God's design.

Since every living thing always reproduces after its own kind, can the harvest that we are talking about today come from the source of abundance?

Through sin, Adam's spirit was disconnected from the very source of life, and he was destined to try to make it through life with his own natural abilities. He went from having access to the infinite source of God's wisdom, revelation, creativity, and imagination to using 6–10 percent of his brain capacity. He no longer had access to the infinite source of God's love, joy, peace, patience, goodness, kindness, gentleness, and self-control. In an instant, he went from God's image, which is love, to the opposite. Some may think that the opposite of love is hate, but biblically, the opposite of agape love (God's love) is self-centeredness.

The effect of sin caused mankind to go from a spiritual man to a natural man. The natural man has a nature that is in opposition to God. Galatians 5:17 says, "For the flesh craves what is contrary to the Spirit."

He went from having access to the infinite source of God's provision to a life of self-effort, from a garden filled with everything he would ever need to hard soil and weeds. He went from having access to the infinite source of God's power to being ruled by Satan's power.

Satan rules mankind by tempting us to live by our fallen nature, satisfying our fleshly desires, even at the expense of others. Think about it. Love prefers others above itself. Love lays down its life for others. Yet look at how Adam answers God's question in Genesis 3:12. "The man said, 'The woman whom you gave to be with me, she gave me fruit of the tree, and I ate.'"

Did Adam protect his wife? Did he put her needs above his own? *No*! The first attitude after the fall was self-centeredness. He blamed God and Eve.

The enemy's blow was severe and complete. He accomplished his mission to steal, kill, and destroy.

God and Satan have the same plan: to establish their own identity in people! Identity is based on your nature, and whoever has the dominant influence over the nature of a culture controls the culture. Any guess on who is winning the influence battle in America today? The enemy is succeeding.

We can look at any social justice issue from the garden until today, and self-centeredness is at the root. Look at the genocide issue. Whether it is aimed at a race, a religion, or the unborn, it is about someone seeing themselves as more valuable or important than another.

Look at the slavery issue. It doesn't matter the time or place in history or how a person is being exploited—whether people were being forced into making pyramids in Egypt, picking cotton in the Carolinas, or being forced into the sex trade—it is simply one person or a group saying, with their words and actions, "My profit or self-satisfaction is more important than someone else's personal dignity or value."

Our identity affects every decision we make. Why do you think the enemy wants to take the creation story out of our schools? For our children to grow up with the belief that they are wonderfully and uniquely made by a loving heavenly Father who established a plan and purpose for them before the foundation of the world is detrimental to Satan's plan.

So let's tell them that they are here by accident, they came from a monkey, or a slime puddle, and in the end, nothing they do will make a difference. This will create a belief system lacking value, hope, and purpose. Then, when they grow up and treat each other in a way that reflects this belief system, we can cause people to question the goodness of God!

All of the issues that are plaguing our world today are simply the effects of man's fallen sin nature and the effects of Satan's influence over the world.

Be of good cheer! Let me give you just a glimpse of hope. God sent Jesus to deal with the effects of sin and destroy the works of Satan so that *all* people can be restored back to his design and intent.

The apostle John testifies about Jesus. "The next day John saw Jesus coming toward him and said, 'Look, the Lamb of God, who takes away the sin of the world!'" (John 1:29). "The reason the Son of God appeared was to destroy the works of the devil" (1 John 3:8b ESV).

CHAPTER 3

I Am Forgiven

WHAT DO YOU think of when you hear the word *forgiveness*? Do you see it only as a ticket to heaven? Or is there more?

When you look at the original languages that the Bible was written in—Hebrew, Greek, and Aramaic—they are all much more complex than our English language. One word can have multiple meanings that reveal important spiritual truths. If we don't understand the meaning of these words, we will miss the benefits of God's promises. You can't believe something that you do not know.

Forgiveness is one of those words that has multiple definitions. It describes different aspects of redemption. Let's take a biblical look at forgiveness: *pardon, deliverance from captivity, remission* (Mounce Reverse-Interlinear New Testament).

1) Pardon: restores our relationship with God.
2) Deliverance: sets us free from the power of Satan.
3) Remission: restores us back to God's image and likeness.

1) Pardon: restores our relationship with God. Pardon is defined as a release from the penalty of an offense; to release (a person) from liability for an offense (Dictionary.com).

Romans 6:23a says, "For the wages of sin is death." God is perfect in love, yet he is also perfect in justice. There was a consequence for disobedience that led to sin, and it was separation from God and, ultimately, death. There was no way for an imperfect person to pay the debt for himself.

Jesus was the sinless sacrifice who became sin for us. He had to be born of a virgin because the nature of sin was passed down through the seed of man. If Jesus was born through the seed of Joseph, he would have the same sin nature as us and would not qualify as our sinless sacrifice. So Jesus was born from the seed of God, just like Adam was before the fall. Luke 1:34–35 says:

> Then Mary said to the angel, "How can this be, since I do not know a man?" And the angel answered and said to her, "The Holy Spirit will come upon you, and the power of the Highest will overshadow you; therefore, also, that Holy One who is to be born will be called the Son of God."

Jesus made that one sacrifice for *all* people, for *all* sin, for *all* time. God reveals the onetime payment that Jesus made that would set us free from the wages of sin forever. "But this Man, after He had offered one sacrifice for sins forever, sat down at the right hand of God" (Hebrews 10:12).

Jesus equated eternal life, not with an eternal destination called heaven but with knowing him and the Father. "Now this is eternal life: that they know you, the only true God, and Jesus Christ, whom you have sent" (John 17:3).

To fully understand this, we have to understand the usage of the word *know* here. Did he mean knowledge as in the attainment of facts and information?

In both the Old and New Testament, the word *know* describes an intimate relationship that produces life. "Now Adam knew Eve his wife, and she conceived and bore Cain, and said, "I have acquired a man from the Lord" (Genesis 4:1). "Then Mary said to the angel, 'How can this be, since I do not know a man?'" (Luke 1:34). Mary was asking the angel how she was going to get pregnant since she has never had an intimate relationship with a man.

The capacity for intimate relationship with God, who is the source of life, has been restored for those who believe. 1 Corinthians

8:6 (AMPC) says, "Yet for us there is [only] one God, the Father, Who is the Source of all things and for Whom we [have life], and one Lord, Jesus Christ, through and by Whom are all things and through and by Whom we [ourselves exist]."

The only way to receive this life is to stay connected to the source. The Bible calls this abiding, and it is one of the major themes in Scripture. John 15:5 (NKJV) states, "I am the vine, you are the branches. He who abides in Me, and I in him, bears much fruit; for without Me you can do nothing."

Relationship is so important to the heart and plan of God that the enemy came up with not just one but two strategies to thwart it.

- Strategy one: deferred hope.

Mary loves kids, and she is part of an after-school ministry that allows her to share the love of Jesus. One day, little Johnny comes in, sits down, opens his lunch box, and begins to eat his afternoon snack. Mary goes over and starts to talk to him about Jesus. She says that God made everything, including him, but there is a problem called sin. Because of God's great love for us, he sent Jesus to remove sin, and she quoted John 3:16. "God has a wonderful plan for you, Johnny, so that your sins can be forgiven, and you can go to heaven someday." She asks Johnny if he would like to follow Jesus. He says yes. She leads him in a prayer to receive Jesus.

Johnny smiles, closes up his lunch box, and says "I am ready."

Mary responds, "Ready for what?"

"Ready to go to heaven," Johnny says.

Mary responds, "Um, uh, well, Johnny, it doesn't work that way."

"What do you mean?" asks Johnny.

"You don't get to go to heaven until you die," Mary says.

"I thought you said that God loves me," Johnny replies.

Mary says, "He does."

Johnny asks, "But he doesn't want to spend time with me until I die?"

Mary breathes out a silent ugh.

I hope you feel the tension in your heart that I feel as I write this because this is the primary way we have shared the Gospel for hundreds of years in America.

So here are some questions we need to answer. When Jesus said, "It is finished," was he talking about a future hope that leaves us separated from intimacy with the Father until we die? Were we to be left under the tyrannical rule of the one who came to steal, kill, and destroy? Were we intended to remain imprisoned by the same self-centered mindset, motives, attitudes, and behaviors that we inherited through the fall?

- Strategy two: knowledge over intimacy.

If we can be honest, most of the focus of the Christian life is built upon the attainment of knowledge about God. We take a very intellectual approach to spiritual growth. We spend endless hours studying about him and precious little time in communion with him.

I knew the first day I met my wife that she was the kind of person I wanted to be with for the rest of my life. Suppose after meeting me she set out on a journey to discover everything she could about me. She even went to Ancestry.com and traced my family tree back to the twelfth century, yet every time I called her to go on a date, she said she was busy. After five calls, I decided she was just not interested in me. Then, one day, I ran into her best friend, and she told me how much Teresa cared for me, that she had spent hundreds of hours researching, studying, and verifying every aspect of my legacy and history.

I guess that would be nice in a creepy, stalking kind of way, but it falls short of what I am looking for, intimacy. The evidence that you love someone is that you want to spend time with them and live in a relationship based on dependency and trust.

2) Deliverance: sets us free from the power of Satan. The same Greek word that is translated as pardoned from sin (forgiveness) is also used here as being delivered from Satan's captivity. Jesus came to set us free from the power of Satan.

> Luke 4:18–19 says, "The Spirit of the Lord is on me, because he has anointed me to proclaim good news to the poor. He has sent me to proclaim *freedom for the prisoners* [emphasis mine] and recovery of sight for the blind, to set the oppressed free."

During Paul's encounter with Jesus on the Damascus road, Jesus tells him what his mission is.

> So I said, "Who are You, Lord?" And He said, "I am Jesus, whom you are persecuting. But rise and stand on your feet; for I have appeared to you for this purpose, to make you a minister and a witness both of the things which you have seen and of the things which I will yet reveal to you. I will deliver you from the Jewish people, as well as from the Gentiles, to whom I now send you, to open their eyes, *in order to turn them from darkness to light, and from the power of Satan to God* [emphasis mine], that they may receive forgiveness of sins and an inheritance among those who are sanctified by faith in Me." (Acts 26:15–19)

Paul was to teach us that Jesus came to open our eyes to the truth that sets us free and reveal the deceptions that are keeping us in darkness and forgive (deliver) us from the power that Satan has over us.

We have to understand that Satan is not all-powerful. As a matter of fact, he can't do anything to you without your consent and cooperation.

The tools he uses to get our cooperation are:

- Deception: The act of causing someone to accept as true or valid what is false or invalid.

"Now the serpent was more crafty than any other beast of the field that the Lord God had made. He said to the woman, 'Did God actually say, "You shall not eat of any tree in the garden?"'" (Genesis 3:1 ESV).

Satan's greatest deception is to convince us that all of the effects of the fall are normal and to be expected.

Everything that God intended for man to experience was perverted through the fall. Love became self-centeredness, joy became sorrow, peace became stress, etc. (refer back to the chapter "Love Lost").

Satan is the one who ultimately controls the airwaves, and in our lifetime, there has been billions of dollars spent to convince you that all of these effects are a normal part of the human experience. What passes for entertainment and even the commercials bombard us with lies. What God says is from the enemy is now being paraded as acceptable or to be expected! Yet none of these conditions existed in the garden before the fall, and they will not exist in heaven, so they can't be God's design for us.

Deliverance from deception comes from knowing the truth. "And you shall know the truth, and the truth shall make you free" (John 8:32). The word *know* is experiential knowledge. God never intended for us to just know facts about doctrine; he wants us to know him, his nature, and how the kingdom works so that we can experience all of the benefits that Jesus paid for.

Paul tells us in 1 Corinthians that the natural mind cannot discern the things of God.

> But God now unveils these profound realities to us by the Spirit. Yes, he has revealed to us his inmost heart and deepest mysteries through the Holy Spirit, who constantly explores all things. After all, who can really see into a person's heart and know his hidden impulses, except for that person's spirit? So it is with God. His thoughts and secrets are only fully understood by his Spirit, the Spirit of God. For we did not receive the spirit

> of this world system but the Spirit of God so that we might come to understand and experience all that grace has lavished upon us. And we articulate these realities with the words imparted to us by the Spirit and not with the words taught by human wisdom. We join together Spirit-revealed truths with Spirit-revealed words. Someone living on an entirely human level rejects the revelations of God's Spirit, for they make no sense to him. He can't understand the revelations of the Spirit because they are only discovered by the illumination of the Spirit. (1 Corinthians 2:10–15 TPT)

When we read this verse, we think that Paul is only talking about a person who is not born again. That is true because a person without the Holy Spirit cannot discern spiritual truths, but it is also possible for born-again Christians to try to interpret Scriptures through their natural mind. That will hinder your ability to receive from God because you have to believe to receive. The problem is your natural mind can only believe what it can see, taste, hear, smell, and feel.

God gave us another tool called faith so that we can believe what we cannot see based on the integrity of God's Word alone. It's not just what you know but also what you believe that sets you free from Satan's deceptions.

In John 20:24–29, Jesus contrasts the difference between natural knowledge and faith.

> Now Thomas, called the Twin, one of the twelve, was not with them when Jesus came. The other disciples therefore said to him, "We have seen the Lord." So he said to them, "*Unless I see in His hands the print of the nails, and put my finger into the print of the nails, and put my hand into His side, I will not believe* [emphasis mine]." And after eight days His disciples were again inside, and

> Thomas with them. Jesus came, the doors being shut, and stood in the midst, and said, "Peace to you!" Then He said to Thomas, "Reach your finger here, and look at My hands; and reach your hand here, and put it into My side. Do not be unbelieving, but believing." And Thomas answered and said to Him, "My Lord and my God!" Jesus said to him, "*Thomas, because you have seen Me, you have believed. Blessed are those who have not seen and yet have believed* [emphasis mine]."

Think about what you were taught growing up: "I will believe it when I see it." That is natural knowledge; the kind that only believes what it can see, taste, hear, smell, and feel. Jesus was saying that the blessed person, the one who receives God's promises is the one that doesn't see yet believes. His faith takes God at His word.

- Accusations.
  - Guilt: the tool he uses to keep you imprisoned because of what you have done to others.
  - Shame: the tool he uses to keep you imprisoned because of what has been done to you.
  - Condemnation: the tool he uses to make you think that you are worthy to be judged and beyond God's capacity to love.

Does God have an answer for this assault on his people? Can we really be free from the influence and accusations of the enemy? The answer is an emphatic yes! "Then I heard a loud voice saying in heaven, 'Now salvation, and strength, and the kingdom of our God, and the power of His Christ have come, for the accuser of our brethren, who accused them before our God day and night, has been cast down'" (Revelation 12:10).

Think of the enemy as a prosecuting attorney. When there is a case before him, his job is to find every shred of evidence against the defendant to prove his guilt. Satan will try to use your past against you! He likes to dwell in your past, bring up your mistakes, faults, failures, and shortcomings, and tell you that you haven't changed and you are still worthy to be judged. Don't take the bait. In John 8:44, Satan is called "the father of lies."

Freedom from accusations

Freedom through Jesus. "He canceled out every legal violation we had on our record and the old arrest warrant that stood to indict us. He erased it all—our sins, our stained soul—he deleted it all and they cannot be retrieved! Everything we once were in Adam has been placed onto his cross and nailed permanently there as a public display of cancellation" (Colossians 2:14 TPT).

"This '*stained soul*' has been erased of its filth. The word '*erased*' explicitly holds the concept of removal of sins. This would mean the nature of Adam has been erased and the nature of Christ has been embedded into us. We are totally free from *every* [emphasis mine] trace of sin by the power of the blood of Jesus Christ" (The Passion Translation).

Praise God! He made a way when there was no way.

The blood of Jesus deleted all evidence—past, present, and future as well as the arrest warrant. He deleted it all. There is nothing left for him to accuse you of. You are free! Romans 8:1–2 says, "Therefore, there is now no condemnation for those who are in Christ Jesus, because through Christ Jesus the law of the Spirit who gives life has set you free from the law of sin and death."

So why do we still struggle with guilt, shame, and condemnation after we are born again?

Here is one reason. We have been taught that one of the roles of the Holy Spirit is to convict us of sin.

> And when He has come, He will convict the world of sin, and of righteousness, and of judg-

> ment: of sin, because they do not believe in Me; of righteousness, because I go to My Father and you see Me no more; of judgment, because the ruler of this world is judged (John 16:8–11).

If you just read verse 8, you get the impression that one of the roles of Holy Spirit is to convict the world of sin, right? Verses 9–11 puts it in context.

The Holy Spirit will convict the world of just one sin, not believing in Jesus. Without believing in Jesus, there is no way to be saved. "That if you confess with your mouth the Lord Jesus and believe in your heart that God has raised Him from the dead, you will be saved" (Romans 10:9).

He convicts the world of righteousness (right standing) by revealing the truth about Jesus's redemptive work. Romans 5:1 (AMP) states, "Therefore, since we are justified (acquitted, declared righteous, and given a right standing with God) through faith, let us [grasp the fact that we] have [the peace of reconciliation to hold and to enjoy] peace with God through our Lord Jesus Christ (the Messiah, the Anointed One)."

It is Satan, not humanity, that is being judged by God. "For God did not send His Son into the world to condemn the world, but that the world through Him might be saved" (John 3:17).

Let me help you understand how to apply this verse. If you believe that the Holy Spirit is causing you to experience guilt, shame, and condemnation, then instead of resisting it as a satanic assault, you will submit to it, which is to come into agreement with. "Therefore submit to God. Resist the devil and he will flee from you" (James 4:7).

Hebrews 10:14–17 says:

> For by one offering He has perfected forever those who are being sanctified. But the Holy Spirit also witnesses to us; for after He had said before, "This is the covenant that I will make with them after those days, says the Lord: I will put My laws into their hearts, and in their minds I will write

> them," then He adds, "*Their sins and their lawless deeds I will remember no more* [emphasis mine]."

If God doesn't remember our sins anymore, how could the Holy Spirit convict us of it?

Jesus exchanged your

- guilt for innocence;
- shame for honor;
- condemnation for acceptance.

3) Remission: restores us back to God's image and likeness. The same Greek word for forgiveness also means remission. Remission is understood as forgiveness or pardon of an offense. It has the effect of putting back the offender into the same situation he was before the commission of the offense (Bible Dictionary.com).

"For this is My blood of the new covenant, which is shed for many for the remission of sins" (Matthew 28:26).

For us to experience remission, two things had to take place.

1) The *nature* of sin had to be removed.

Let's look at the most famous passage on redemption. In Isaiah 53, the prophet Isaiah prophesied about the atoning work of Jesus. Atonement means "to stand as an equivalent, to make reparation, amends, or satisfaction for an offense or a crime, by which reconciliation is made between the offended and the offending parties."

Isaiah 53:12 (Amplified Bible) states, "Therefore, I will divide and give Him a portion with the great [kings and rulers], And He shall divide the spoils with the mighty, Because He [willingly] poured out His life to death, And was counted among the transgressors; Yet He Himself *bore and took away the sin* [emphasis mine] of many, And interceded [with the Father] for the transgressors."

What Isaiah is telling us is that Jesus became our sin substitute, our atonement. He took upon himself the nature of sin that came through Adam and carried it away forever, for all time, and exchanged it for his perfect nature.

It is not an accident that most of the words used to describe the atoning work of Jesus start with the prefix *re*, meaning back or again. Look at some of these words: *reborn, redeemed, remission.* These words carry with them the connotation of returning us to God's original design for mankind, his image and likeness.

Here is how Paul describes God dealing with our sin nature. Romans 6:5–7 says:

> For if we have been united together in the likeness of His death, certainly we also shall be in the likeness of His resurrection, knowing this, that our old man was crucified with Him, that the body of sin might be done away with, that we should no longer be slaves of sin. For he who has died has been freed from sin.

In the Greek, the words *united together* means to grow in union or to plant in union. It describes two plants that are growing together, closely entwined, or even united. It speaks of our union together in Christ's death. Spiritually speaking, when Jesus died, your old man with its sin nature died. When he resurrected, you were joined together in his resurrection life a new creation.

What does it mean that he who has died is free from sin?

Suppose you walked into a graveyard and began to stomp on a grave, kicking, spitting, and cussing at the headstone. Is there any chance that the person in the grave would be tempted to become angry?

What if you talked to that person about a global pandemic? Would he be tempted to become fearful?

What if you told him about an upcoming financial recession, would he be tempted to become anxious?

What if it was a man in the grave, and a beautiful young woman walked up and began to proposition him with sexual favors, would he be tempted to lust?

The answer to all of these questions is *no*! Why? *Because he is dead*!

God never intended to try to modify your old nature. It was too far gone. It had to be killed off and replaced with the sinless nature of Jesus.

2) The second part of remission is to give us a new nature.

The moment you were born again, you became a new creation *in Christ*. "Therefore, if anyone is in Christ, he is a new creation; old things have passed away; behold, all things have become new" (2 Corinthians 5:17).

If you are born again, you *are* in Christ! Old things have (past tense accomplishment) passed away, and all things have (past tense accomplishment) become new. This is describing your born-again experience.

Let's let the apostle Paul drive this truth home. "I have been crucified with Christ; it is no longer I who live, but Christ lives in me; and the life which I now live in the flesh I live by faith in the Son of God, who loved me and gave Himself for me" (Galatians 2:20).

Do you see it? Paul is saying that his old man with the nature of Adam was crucified with Jesus, and now the nature of Christ is living in him.

After your old nature was dealt with through the death, burial, and resurrection of Jesus, he sat down at the right hand of God and sent us the Holy Spirit to conform us into the image of his Son. "But I tell you the truth, it is to your advantage that I go away; for if I do not go away, the Helper will not come to you; but if I go, I will send Him to you" (John 16:7 NASB).

When you are born again, your spirit and God's Spirit become one in Christ. "But he who is joined to the Lord is one spirit with Him (Corinthians 6:17). "At that day you will know that I am in My Father, and you in Me, and I in you" (John 14:20).

"What a glorious relationship that we have *now* [emphasis mine] with God! Christ is dwelling in the Father; we are dwelling in Christ; Christ is dwelling in us; the Father is dwelling in us. How beautiful it is!" (*Smith's Bible Commentary*).

In the Epistles, Paul uses the phrases *in Christ*, *in whom*, and *in Him* over a 140 times to describe what it means to be conformed into the image of God.

"For in Him the whole fullness of Deity (the Godhead) continues to dwell in bodily form [giving complete expression of the divine nature]. And you are in Him, made full and having come to fullness of life [in Christ you too are filled with the Godhead—Father, Son and Holy Spirit—and reach full spiritual stature]. And He is the Head of all rule and authority [of every angelic principality and power]" (Colossians 2:9–10 AMPC).

You are not waiting to get to heaven to experience God's new creation. The moment you are born again, Jesus exchanges the nature that came through Adam with all of the effects of sin and exchanges it for the perfect nature of Jesus with all of the benefits of the new creation life!

Through the remission of your sin, you have received the fullness of the

- mind of Christ.

"For 'who has known the mind of the Lord that he may instruct Him?' But we have the mind of Christ" (1 Corinthians 2:16).

- nature of Christ.

> But the fruit produced by the Holy Spirit within you is divine love in all its varied expressions: joy that overflows, peace that subdues, patience that endures, kindness in action, a life full of virtue, faith that prevails, gentleness of heart, and strength of spirit. Never set the law above

> these qualities, for they are meant to be limitless. (Galatians 5:22–23 TPT)

- power of Christ.

> The eyes of your understanding being enlightened; that you may know what is the hope of His calling, what are the riches of the glory of His inheritance in the saints, 19 and what is the exceeding greatness of His power toward us who believe, according to the working of His mighty power 20 which He worked in Christ when He raised Him from the dead and seated Him at His right hand in the heavenly places. (Ephesians 1:18–20)

Paul said it this way: "For God has not given us a spirit of fear, but of power and of love and of a sound mind" (2 Timothy 1:7).

Another of Satan's deceptions is to convince us that we are forgiven but still have the same nature, destined to live in bondage to sin and Satan.

"Beware that no one distracts you or intimidates you in their attempt to lead you away from Christ's fullness by pretending to be full of wisdom when they're filled with endless arguments of human logic. For they operate with humanistic and clouded judgments based on the mindset of this world system, and not the anointed truths of the Anointed One" (Colossians 2:8 TPT).

Satan's strategy

Convince the church that forgiveness is limited to paying the price for us to experience the future hope of heaven while leaving us in bondage to the effects of sin and Satan.

CHAPTER 4

I Am a Person of Faith

MATTHEW 9:29 SAYS, "Then He touched their eyes, saying, 'According to your faith let it be to you.'"

Faith defined. Hebrews 11:1a (AMP) states, "Now faith is the assurance (title deed, confirmation) of things hoped for (divinely guaranteed) and the evidence of things not seen [the conviction of their reality—faith comprehends as fact what cannot be experienced by the physical senses]."

Let me sum this up in one easy statement: "Faith is the divine ability to believe and act upon what you believe."

Two types of faith

1) Natural faith: This is the God-given faith that we use to function in this natural world we call earth. Here our faith is established based on our natural senses—what we can see, taste, hear, smell, and feel. This kind of faith only functions if it has tangible evidence.

Let me illustrate: Let's say that I was sitting on a dining room chair, and I encouraged you to pull the other chair close and sit down so we could talk. The first thing that would happen would be that subconsciously, you would examine the chair, you would make sure it had four legs, and that it had a stable place to sit on. What you *saw* would give you the natural faith to believe that the chair would hold your weight. But faith also requires an act of your will. The only true measure of faith is if you sit on the chair. Faith believes and acts upon what you believe.

What if I pointed to a chair that only had the two front legs, and the back of the chair was leaning against the wall, and I told you to pull it over and sit on it. Would you have faith to sit on it? No, you would have to *see* that it had four legs and a place to sit before you could believe because natural faith has to have tangible evidence before it can believe.

2) Spiritual faith: This is the faith that God gave us to function in the spiritual unseen. We have to understand that there is more than just this natural world.

The spiritual world preceeded the natural world. Hebrews 11:3 (NET) states, "By faith we understand that the worlds were set in order at God's command, so that the visible has its origin in the invisible." The visible world we call the universe came forth from the invisible world of the Spirit. The origin of the natural is the spiritual. Or you could say that the spiritual is the parent force, and the parent force is greater than what came forth from it.

The spiritual world is also eternal. Second Corinthians 4:18 says, "While we look not at the things which are seen, but at the things which are not seen: for the things which are seen are temporal; but the things which are not seen are eternal."

God gave us spiritual faith to function in the spiritual world. Spiritual faith is established by trusting the truth of God's Word, based on his unchanging nature, and then acting on the truth of God's Word.

The two sides of spiritual faith

For most of my Christian life, I wrestled with understanding the difference between belief and faith. Most dictionaries and even biblical commentaries describe them the same way but, many times, when people came to Jesus to receive, he would speak about belief and faith as if they had two separate functions.

Spiritual faith is like a coin. It has two sides. On one side, we have belief, and belief is the divine ability to take God at his word without any tangible evidence. The other side of the coin is faith or acting upon what you believe.

Matthew 9:27–31 says:

> When Jesus departed from there, two blind men followed Him, crying out and saying, "Son of David, have mercy on us!" And when He had come into the house, the blind men came to Him. And Jesus said to them, "*Do you believe* [emphasis mine] that I am able to do this?" They said to Him, "Yes, Lord." Then He touched their eyes, saying, "*According to your faith* [emphasis mine] let it be to you." And their eyes were opened. And Jesus sternly warned them, saying, "See that no one knows it." But when they had departed, they spread the news about Him in all that country.

These blind men believed that Jesus was able to heal them because they heard that he was the healer and everyone who came to him got healed.

There also had to be a component of faith or acting upon what they believed. Their faith was revealed by simply coming to Jesus, expecting to receive.

The purpose of faith

Faith allows us to believe an unseen spiritual reality. Hebrews 11:1b (AMP) states, "And the evidence of things not seen [the conviction of their reality—faith comprehends as fact what cannot be experienced by the physical senses]."

John 6:63 says, "It is the Spirit who gives life; the flesh profits nothing. The words that I speak to you are spirit, and they are life."

Jesus is telling us that his Word is spiritual and is revealing spiritual reality.

When you try to use your natural faith to believe a spiritual reality, the Bible calls it carnality. Carnality simply means to be controlled by your natural senses.

Romans 8:6 states, "For to be carnally minded is death, but to be spiritually minded is life and peace."

Carnal mindedness leads to death because you have no capacity to believe something unless it is proceeded by physical evidence.

Spiritual mindedness leads to life because it allows you to believe what you cannot see based on the integrity of God's nature and Word.

Why is this important? According to Jesus, you have to believe that you have something first, then you will have it. Mark 11:24 states, "Therefore I say to you, whatever things you ask when you pray, believe that you receive them, and you will have them."

One of the greatest strategies of the enemy is to convince us to use our natural faith to try to receive a spiritual reality.

Before we can get a greater understanding about faith, we need to understand the difference between faith and hope.

Hope is always future tense. Hope is a feeling of desire and expectation that things will go well in the future (*Collins English Dictionary*).

Colossians 1:5 states, "Because of the hope which is laid up for you in heaven, of which you heard before in the word of the truth of the gospel."

Titus 2:13 says, "looking for the blessed hope and glorious appearing of our great God and Savior Jesus Christ."

Think about how the air conditioner works in your house. You come home at the end of a hot summer day, and it is eighty-six degrees in your house, so you turn your thermostat to seventy-six degrees because that is your desired temperature, what you hope your house will feel like soon. There is a second component in your AC system. It is called the pump. It is what produces the cold air that will bring the desired temperature into reality. Without the pump, it doesn't matter how low you set the temperature or how much you hope your house will feel cooler; nothing will happen!

Faith is present tense: now faith is! Faith is the title, deed, or guarantee that brings our hopes into a present-tense reality.

Faith is a grace gift

Ephesians 2:8–9 says, "For by grace you have been saved through faith, and that not of yourselves; it is the gift of God, 9 not of works, lest anyone should boast."

This verse reveals one of the great truths in Christianity, that salvation is a grace gift. We are saved because of what Jesus did, not because of anything we could do. Contained in this verse is another great biblical truth. Faith is also a grace gift.

Everyone was born with natural faith, the kind that only believes what it can see, taste, hear, smell, and feel.

For you to receive the great gift of salvation, you had to believe something that you had never seen or experienced. You had to believe things that you never saw; that a virgin gave birth to a son, he lived a sinless life, was arrested, beaten, crucified, buried, and rose again, and is now alive in heaven, interceding to the Father on your behalf.

God loves you so much he gave you the gift of faith so that you could believe what Jesus did so that you could receive the gift of salvation.

The measure of faith

There was an interview with a German evangelist named Reinhard Bonnke. He ministered in Africa for over thirty years and reached millions of people with the Gospel. He was known for having large outdoor crusades, his largest event had over 1.6 million in attendance. His preaching would always be confirmed with signs and wonders, and it was normal to see hundreds of people get healed from diseases or delivered from demonic oppression. During this interview, an American journalist asked him a question. "Is the reason that we don't see consistent miracles in America is because we don't have enough faith?"

He said, "No, the reason is that Americans believe there are different levels of faith."

Romans 12:3 (KJV) states, "For I say, through the grace given unto me, to every man that is among you, not to think of himself more highly than he ought to think; but to think soberly, according as God hath dealt to every man *the measure of faith* [emphasis mine]."

Everyone was given the same measure of faith to believe the impossible. He doesn't give some a ladle, another a cup, and yet another a teaspoon. We all receive the same measure of faith.

We received the faith of Jesus

Galatians 2:16 says, "Knowing that a man is not justified by the works of the law, but by the faith of Jesus Christ, even we have believed in Jesus Christ, that we might be justified by the faith of Christ, and not by the works of the law: for by the works of the law shall no flesh be justified."

Paul says that we are justified by the faith *of* Christ.

Galatians 2:20 states, "I am crucified with Christ: nevertheless I live; yet not I, but Christ liveth in me: and the life which I now live in the flesh I live by the faith of the Son of God, who loved me, and gave himself for me."

Paul also said that his new creation life is lived by the faith *of* the Son of God.

Second Peter 1:1 (AMP) says, "Simon Peter, a bond-servant and apostle (special messenger, personally chosen representative) of Jesus Christ, To those who have received and possess [by God's will] a precious faith of the same kind as ours, by the righteousness of our God and Savior, Jesus Christ."

Peter is writing to the church and telling us that we all possess the same faith as him, which is the faith *of* Jesus.

- When you got born again, you received the same faith that Jesus used to calm a storm, cast out devils, cleanse lepers, heal the sick, and raise the dead.

- You have the same faith that Paul used in Ephesus when people took his handkerchiefs and laid them on people, and they were healed or delivered.
- You have the same faith that Peter had when his shadow healed people in Jerusalem.

The truth is we don't have a faith problem, we have a knowledge problem. We can't believe a truth that we don't know or our faith is based on a misunderstanding of scripture. If you have been taught that miracles ceased with the apostles, you will not have faith for miracles.

Faith comes by hearing

Romans 10:17 states, "So then faith comes by hearing, and hearing by the word of God."

For anyone to receive the gift of salvation, they have to first hear the Word of God. Many people got saved, just from hearing the promise in John 3:16.

Every promise of God carries the seed of faith to receive *that* promise. A seed always produces after its own kind. John 3:16 carries the seed of faith needed to receive the promise of eternal life. If you believe that eternal life means going to heaven, that is what you will have faith to receive. The promise of Ephesians 1:3—"Blessed be the God and Father of our Lord Jesus Christ, who has blessed us with every spiritual blessing in the heavenly places in Christ"—carries the faith seed to receive all spiritual blessings. Each promise of God carries the faith seed to reproduce *that* specific promise.

God is supernatural; therefore, all of his promises are supernatural. Satan knows that you already have all the faith you need to receive every supernatural promise, and it is all based on what you believe about God's Word. His game plan is to get us to wrongly interpret God's Word.

Faith comes by hearing the Word of God but is dependent on how you interpret Scripture.

Two types of knowledge

1. Natural knowledge.

Second Corinthians 2:14 (DLNT) states, "But a natural person does not accept the things of the Spirit of God. For they are foolishness to him and he is not able to understand, because they are spiritually examined."

When we read this scripture, we usually think that Paul is talking only about an unsaved man, but it is also possible for saved people to try to interpret the Scriptures using their natural knowledge.

Using natural knowledge to interpret the Bible has two adverse effects.

a) Your natural mind uses logic and reason and is designed to gather and understand facts, principles, laws, and theories. That is great if you are studying to be an engineer or a doctor because that requires intellectual knowledge. The Bible is an autobiography. It is God revealing his true nature to man so that they would desire a relationship with him.

The Pharisees knew every law, every doctrine, every biblical principle, yet they were lacking the one thing they needed most to know the Father. John 18:19 states, "Jesus answered, 'You know neither Me nor My Father. If you had known Me, you would have known My Father also.'"

b) Your natural mind cannot believe anything that can't be explained through your natural senses. If you can't see it, taste it, hear it, smell it, or feel it, you can't accept it as truth. So you either have to reject it or create a theology to support your experience or lack thereof.

Here is an example: A couple of years ago, my wife and I were watching a documentary on the Exodus story, and there were two theological professors who were being interviewed. Everything was going well until they got to the Red Sea. Their statement: "Most biblical maps lead us to believe that the place we are standing is the place where the children of Israel crossed, but that would be impossible. The water is just too deep." Then they went on to explain that if you go thirty miles to the south, the Red Sea turns into a marsh (the Reed Sea) and that is where the crossing happened, in ankle-deep water.

Logic will always deny the supernatural because it can't be explained. Even if their theory was true, it would still be a miracle; this means that Pharaoh's army, with its horses and chariots, all drowned in ankle-deep water. What they are doing is conforming God's Word to what they believe, instead of conforming what they believe to God's Word. Natural knowledge does not produce faith. The truth is, as hard as we try, we cannot explain away a supernatural God.

Food for thought: To reject the supernatural is to reject God because God is supernatural.

We need to heed the warning of Paul. Colossians 2:8 (AMPC) says, "See to it that no one carries you off as spoil or makes you yourselves captive by his so-called philosophy and intellectualism and vain deceit (idle fancies and plain nonsense), following *human tradition (men's ideas of the material rather than the spiritual world), just crude notions following the rudimentary and elemental teachings of the universe and disregarding [the teachings of] Christ (the Messiah)* [emphasis mine]."

Satan wants you to use your intellect to convince you that you are confined to this natural world where we are dominated by all of the effects of the fall, and that not until you die do you have access to the spiritual world with all of its benefits.

2. Spiritual knowledge.

First Corinthians 2:11–13 (TPT) states:

> His thoughts and secrets are only fully understood by his Spirit, the Spirit of God. For we did not receive the spirit of this world system but the

> Spirit of God, so that we might come to understand and experience all that grace has lavished upon us. And we articulate these realities with the words imparted to us by the Spirit and not with the words taught by human wisdom. We join together Spirit-revealed truths with Spirit-revealed words.

The apostle Paul is telling us that the thoughts and secrets of this supernatural God can only be understood by spiritual knowledge. God gave us spiritual knowledge so that we can understand and experience all of God's redemptive promises. When we interpret God's Word through spiritual knowledge, the truth of God's Word carries the seed of faith necessary to believe and receive every promise of God.

The Word of God is described in two ways.

a) Logos: the divinely inspired, written Word of God
b) Rhema: the divinely revealed, spoken Word of God.

Now let's go back and look at Romans 10:17, which states, "So then faith comes by hearing, and hearing by the word of God."

If you read this in the Greek, it says faith comes by hearing the rhema Word of Christo. The word *Christo* means anointed. To be exact, faith comes by hearing the anointed, divinely revealed, spoken Word of God. This is talking about when the Holy Spirit reveals the anointed revealed Word of God into your heart.

Let me illustrate this in scripture. Matthew 16:13–19 says:

> When Jesus came into the region of Caesarea Philippi, He asked His disciples, saying, "Who do men say that I, the Son of Man, am?" So they said, "Some say John the Baptist, some Elijah, and others Jeremiah or one of the prophets." He said to them, "But who do you say that I am?" Simon Peter answered and said, "You are the Christ, the

> Son of the living God." Jesus answered and said to him, "Blessed are you, Simon Bar-Jonah, for flesh and blood has not revealed this to you, but My Father who is in heaven. And I also say to you that you are Peter, and on this rock I will build My church, and the gates of Hades shall not prevail against it.

Jesus knew that people had many opinions about who they thought he was, so he asked his disciples who they thought he was, and probably, as usual, impetuous Peter was the first one to answer. This time, he got it right. "You are the Christ, the Son of the living God."

Here is what we need to see. Jesus said this was not revealed by flesh and blood. In other words, this was not natural head knowledge. This was an anointed, divine revelation (rhema Word) that God downloaded into Peter's heart.

Now follow me. Many people teach that the rock that Jesus was going to build his church upon was Peter (Petra, little rock). I believe that the rock that the church is supposed to be built on is the rhema; anointed, divinely inspired Word that the Holy Spirit speaks to your heart.

According to Jesus, belief is the key to receiving from him. Mark 9:23 says, "Jesus said to him, "If you can believe, all things are possible to him who believes."

Where does the Bible say that belief comes from? Romans 10:10 states, "For with the heart one believes unto righteousness, and with the mouth confession is made unto salvation."

Faith does not come from your head. It comes from your heart. So how do we get God's Word into our hearts?

The main way that God intended for you to establish your heart on the Word of God is through meditation. Proverbs 4:20–22 states,

> My son, give attention to my words; Incline your ear to my sayings. Do not let them depart from your eyes; Keep them in the midst of your heart;

> For they are life to those who find them, And health to all their flesh.

When you develop the habit of meditating on God's Word, making it a priority, keeping your eyes and heart focused on it, the cares of this world will begin to subside, and you will receive the anointed rhema, the divinely inspired Word into your heart that God has been to trying to give you all along. Then all things will be possible.

Here is an important truth and one of the reasons we may not be receiving all of the promises of God. What you believe is not always what comes out of your mouth. We have a public persona that we are trying to project. We want to be seen as people of faith, so we make faith declarations, quote scriptures, and use Christian clichés. What you truly believe is what your heart says to you when no one else is listening.

You can stand up in public and say, "I am more than a conqueror" until you are blue in the face, but when you are all alone, what your heart says is that you just never seem to win, that is what you truly believe and what you will receive.

God loves us so much, and he wants us to receive every redemptive promise that has already been paid for, but we have to decide what we put in our hearts.

Faith works through the law of conception

To understand the law of conception, we have to go back to God's original design for us.

Genesis 1:27–28 (NKJV) says:

> So God created man in His own image; in the image of God He created him; male and female He created them. Then God blessed them, and God said to them, "Be fruitful and multiply; fill the earth and subdue it; have dominion over the

> fish of the sea, over the birds of the air, and over every living thing that moves on the earth."

The first promise that God made to man was that he had blessed them. The Hebrew word means to evoke divine favor to increase.

What was the purpose of this blessing? To be fruitful and multiply. God is a God of abundance so everything he does brings increase.

How did God intend for his creation to increase? He provided a seed. Every living thing comes forth from a seed. A seed works off a law. It is irrefutable and unchanging. Here is the law: every seed reproduces after its own kind. Human seeds produce humans, lemon seeds reproduce lemons, cow seeds reproduce cows.

Every seed has to go through a process called conception. So God had to create a place for this conception to take place. Mammals have a place in their bodies where a seed can be conceived; for a plant, that place is the soil.

I want you to see where God directed his blessings. Deuteronomy 7:13 states, "And He will love you and bless you and multiply you; He will also bless the fruit of your womb and the fruit of your land, your grain and your new wine and your oil, the increase of your cattle and the offspring of your flock, in the land of which He swore to your fathers to give you."

God directed his blessing to the places where his seeds would be conceived. He gave them divine favor to increase.

Let's put this all together now. God gave us seeds that will always produce after their own kind, and a place of conception that was designed for divine increase. That is the law of conception.

The question is, what does the law of conception have to do with our receiving from God?

The Bible clearly teaches that belief is the key to receiving from God. Mark 9:23 (NKJV) says, "Jesus said to him, 'If you can believe, all things are possible to him who believes.'"

I want to teach you an amazing biblical truth about how God designed us to receive from him, and if you will learn and apply this, it will change your life forever.

The Bible teaches that words produce thoughts that shape our belief. Psalm 23:7 (MEV) states, "For as he thinks in his heart, so is he."

We usually associate thinking with our minds; therefore, what we believe is stored in our heads.

The Bible paints a different picture. It ties our thinking to our hearts and says that our heart is where belief is formed. Proverbs 4:20–23 (NLT) says:

> My child, pay attention to what I say. Listen carefully to my words. Don't lose sight of them. Let them penetrate deep into your heart, for they bring life to those who find them, and healing to their whole body. Guard your heart above all else, for it determines the course of your life.

King Solomon, the wisest man who ever lived is telling us that when you meditate on God's words, they penetrate your heart and paint an image according to the promise, and whatever is conceived in your heart will be produced in your life.

Two sources of thought, two different results

Both God and Satan know that words produce thoughts that shape your belief, and you will have what you believe.

God's words produce thoughts that will always produce abundance.

Satan's words produce thoughts that will always produce destruction.

These thoughts paint a picture or image of you in your heart, and that is what shapes what you believe about yourself. If you want to change your belief, you have to change the image that you have of yourself.

You cannot control every thought that comes into your mind, but you have a choice as to what you allow in your heart. Just like you can't keep a bird from flying over your head, but you can keep it from nesting in your hair.

For a thought to make it from your head to your heart, it has to be focused or meditated on. And whatever thought you allow in your heart will create a belief that will produce a result based on the source of the thought. Matthew 12:35 says, "A good man out of the good treasure of his heart brings forth good things, and an evil man out of the evil treasure brings forth evil things."

Let me illustrate: suppose you are a gardener, and you have a potting shed. Inside of your shed, you have a butcher-block counter that you work on. It is time to plant, so you grab your seeds and pots filled with soil, and you begin to plant the seeds into the soil. If one seed falls out onto the counter, will that seed grow? No, it has to have the right environment, which is found in the soil. Your head is like the counter, your heart is like the soil.

The law of conception

Whatever words you allow in your heart will always produce after the source of the thought.

A law is something that is constant and irrefutable. It works the same way every time.

Think of the law of gravity. It doesn't care whether you live in the northern or southern hemisphere. It doesn't care what race you are, how tall you are, or whether you are rich or poor. If you step off a three-story balcony, the law of gravity is going to work, and it is not going to end well for you.

Jesus teaches a parable that introduces the law of conception.

The parable of the growing seed

Mark 4:26–29 states:

> And he said, So is the kingdom of God, as if a man should cast seed into the ground; And should sleep, and rise night and day, and the seed

> should spring and grow up, he knoweth not how. For the earth bringeth forth fruit of herself; first the blade, then the ear, after that the full corn in the ear. But when the fruit is brought forth, immediately he putteth in the sickle, because the harvest is come.

As we unpack this parable, you need to keep in mind that Jesus is teaching us how he intended for everyone to receive his promises.

Let's break down the parable of the growing seed, verse by verse.

Verse 26 says: "And he said, 'So is the kingdom of God, as if a man should cast seed into the ground.'"

We have to start by understanding what the seed refers to. Jesus is teaching us the seed represents the Word of God. Mark 4:14 states, "The sower sows the word." One of the Greek words for seed is *sporos*: it means semen, seed, sperm.

Here is the law: God's Word is a seed that reproduces after its own kind.

Let's look at a familiar passage so that you can understand what Jesus is teaching about the power of the Word. Isaiah 55:10–11 says:

> The rain and snow come down from the heavens and stay on the ground to water the earth. They cause the grain to grow, producing seed for the farmer and bread for the hungry. It is the same with my word. I send it out, and *it always produces fruit* [emphasis mine]. *It will accomplish* [emphasis mine] all I want it to, and *it will prosper* [emphasis mine] everywhere I send it.

Do you see it? The Word of God will always produce, always accomplish, and always prosper.

Every promise of God contains the faith seed to produce after its own kind.

Verse 27 states, "And should sleep, and rise night and day, and the seed should spring and grow up, he knoweth not how."

This describes the fact that a seed has to stay in the ground long enough to germinate. This is a picture of biblical meditation. I want to be very clear here. Many people think of emptying their mind when they think about meditation. That is based on new age religions. Biblical meditation is to fill your heart with the Word of God. Joshua 1:8 states, "This Book of the Law shall not depart from your mouth, but you shall meditate in it day and night, that you may observe to do according to all that is written in it. For then you will make your way prosperous, and then you will have good success."

Meditation is how you paint a picture in your heart of who God says you are, and when that picture becomes clear enough, it will always become a physical reality.

Do you think that the first time Leonardo da Vinci saw the portrait of *Mona Lisa* was when he finished his last brush stroke and put down his brush? No way! He thought about her, meditated on her until every detail became clear in his heart, then when every detail became clear, he painted what already existed in his heart or imagination onto a canvas for the whole world to enjoy.

Verse 28 says, "For the earth bringeth forth fruit of herself; first the blade, then the ear, after that the full corn in the ear."

Every seed needs not only time but also a place for conception. In this parable, Jesus says that the seed goes into the earth. Notice how he describes the earth. Mark 4:28a says, "For the earth *bringeth forth fruit of herself* [emphasis mine]." Jesus uses the feminine term *herself* to describe the earth because it is the womb where every plant seed is conceived. In the Greek, "of herself" is translated *automatos*, which is where we get our word *automatic*. God made soil and blessed it so that it would conceive the seed automatically. The soil contains every nutrient necessary to conceive whatever seed is planted.

The soil or earth in this parable represents our heart. It is our reproductive womb. Proverbs 4:23 (CSB) states, "Guard your heart above all else, for it is the source of life." Do you see the picture?

Our heart is the soil that germinates the seed automatically until it produces a harvest.

There is an important distinction we have to understand about the soil, whether it is describing the earth or your heart.

Your heart will produce whatever seed is planted.

Think of your garden. The soil doesn't know the difference between a weed seed and a tomato seed. It will germinate whatever seed is planted.

Verse 28b says, "First the blade, then the ear, after that the full corn in the ear."

Jesus wants to remind us that every harvest takes time. In the natural, you don't put a tomato seed in the ground today and enjoy tomatoes tomorrow. This is one thing we wrestle with in our microwave society where we barely have patience to wait for fast food. Whether it is a natural seed or a biblical promise, there is always going to be an element of time.

Verse 29 states, "But when the fruit is brought forth, immediately he putteth in the sickle, because the harvest is come."

Once the fruit is ready, it has to be harvested. Your faith is the key to reaping your harvest.

According to Jesus, your faith is voice activated. Matthew 17:20b says, "I say to you, if you have faith as a mustard seed, *you will say* [emphasis mine] to this mountain, 'Move from here to there,' and it will move; and nothing will be impossible for you."

Philemon 6 says, "That the sharing of your faith may become effective by the acknowledgment of every good thing which is in you in Christ Jesus." Acknowledge: to own or admit to be true by a declaration.

Your spiritual harvest will become a physical reality when you meditate on and declare the truths that are already in you through Christ.

Every seed always reproduces after its own kind. Whatever promise you want to experience in your life, take the promises like a seed, and meditate on them until they paint a picture in your heart.

Whatever you believe in your heart and confess with your mouth will come to pass. Romans 10:9–10 states:

> That if you confess with your mouth the Lord Jesus and believe in your heart that God has raised Him from the dead, you will be saved. For with the heart one believes unto righteousness, and with the mouth confession is made unto salvation.

Understanding God's part and our part in this parable

One of the keys to the law of seed, time, and harvest is knowing what part is God's and what part is ours.

- God provides the seed (the seed is the Word of God).

God's Word will always produce after its own kind.

- We are responsible to sow the seed.

What you do with the seed is totally up to you.

- God is responsible to produce the harvest.

God created your heart to automatically produce whatever seed is sown.

- We are responsible to reap the harvest.

Just like your tomatoes don't fall off the vine and roll into your kitchen when you make a salad, the harvest of God's promises requires us to use our faith.

Here are some questions to ponder.

You have a friend that has a five-hundred-acre ranch, and he calls you and asks you if you will pray in agreement with him that he will have a great harvest this year.

"Again I say to you that if two of you agree on earth concerning anything that they ask, it will be done for them by My Father in heaven" (Matthew 18:19).

When you ask him what kind of seeds he planted, he said he didn't plant any seeds. He was just trusting God for a harvest. Would you have faith to agree with him? Of course not. Everyone knows that if you want to harvest, you have to plant seeds.

According to the law of seed, time, and harvest, the same thing is true with God's promises; you can't expect God to give you a harvest when you never planted seeds.

If you plant corn seeds, they will always produce a harvest of corn. It doesn't matter whether you plant God's seeds or Satan's seeds, what are they going to produce? They will produce whatever you planted because every seed reproduces after its own kind.

You can't plant Satan's seeds and expect God's harvest.

What if you plant corn seeds, then pray for tomatoes? You will reap corn. God never violates his spiritual laws, even if we pray!

How Abraham conceived his promise

In Genesis 12, God promises Abram that he will make him into a great nation. Genesis 12:1–3 says:

> The Lord had said to Abram, "Leave your native country, your relatives, and your father's family, and go to the land that I will show you. I will make you into a great nation. I will bless you and make you famous, and you will be a blessing to others. I will bless those who bless you and curse those who treat you with contempt. All the families on earth will be blessed through you."

The problem is that he was already seventy-five and his wife, Sarai, was sixty-five, and she was barren. This natural knowledge caused him to see himself as childless. Genesis 15:2–3 states:

> But Abram said, "Lord God, what will You give me, seeing I go childless, and the heir of my house is Eliezer of Damascus?" Then Abram said, "Look, You have given me no offspring; indeed one born in my house is my heir!"

Conceiving the Word

For the promise to be fulfilled, God had to do something that would cause Abram to see himself as a father.

Genesis 15:5 says, "Then He brought him outside and said, 'Look now toward heaven, and count the stars if you are able to number them.' And He said to him, 'So shall your descendants be.'"

Genesis 22:17 states, "Blessing I will bless you, and multiplying I will multiply your descendants as the stars of the heaven and as the sand which is on the seashore; and your descendants shall possess the gate of their enemies."

God once again affirmed the promise, yet he didn't stop there. He took him out to the night sky and told him to focus on the stars, then by day, he told him to focus on the sand, and he said both the sand and the stars represent the nation that he would father. Here is the connection we need to see. When God spoke to Joshua about meditating on God's Word, he said to do it night and day, and then it would produce the promise. God's plan for Abram to see himself as a father was to meditate on the promise, both night (stars) and day (sand).

Reaping the harvest

When it was time to reap the harvest, God took him to the next step. Genesis 17:1–5 says:

> When Abram was ninety-nine years old, the Lord appeared to Abram and said to him, "I am Almighty God; walk before Me and be blameless. And I will make My covenant between Me and you, and will multiply you exceedingly." Then Abram fell on his face, and God talked with him, saying: "As for Me, behold, My covenant is with you, and you shall be a father of many nations. No longer shall your name be called Abram, but your name shall be Abraham; for I have made you a father of many nations."

To understand the significance of the name change, we have to understand an important faith principle. We have to see how God exercised his faith. Romans 4:17 states, "As it is written, 'I have made you a father of many nations' in the presence of Him whom he believed—God, who gives life to the dead and calls those things which do not exist as though they did."

God releases his faith through words. When he wants to create something he calls what does not exist as though it did. Hebrews 11:3 (CEV) says, "Because of our faith, we know that the world was made at God's command. We also know that what can be seen was made out of what cannot be seen."

When God was ready to create the stars, he spoke to the firmament and called them forth. When he was ready for animals, he spoke to the earth and called them forth. When he was ready for mankind, he spoke to himself and created us from his image.

Abraham was ninety-nine at this time, and Sarah was eighty-nine. In the natural, ninety-nine-year-old men don't usually father children. Sarah could not conceive when she was in her twenties, and remember, there was only one Immaculate Conception. A miracle was going to have to take place for this to happen, and God was going to use his Word (seed) to produce the promise.

Up to this point, even though he was starting to see himself as a father, and God made a covenant with him that he would be a father. Abraham could continue to confess the words (seeds) "I am childless." These words are in opposition to the promise of God. Stop and ask yourself a question, who is the author of those thoughts? Satan's words are always in direct opposition with God's words because he knows that the law of conception is "every word reproduces after its own kind." Even though God is sovereign (all-powerful), he never violates his laws, even to keep his covenant.

One of the greatest deceptions that we have bought into is that sovereignty means that God's will comes about automatically, but that is not true. Remember the promise that God made to Israel, that he gave them a land flowing with milk and honey. Was the promised land God's will? Did the first generation enter in? I thought God's will came about automatically.

Here is what God said. Numbers 14:28 (CSB) states, "Tell them: As I live—this is the Lord's declaration—*I will do to you exactly as I heard you say* [emphasis mine]."

Now ask yourself what they were saying. Ten times in the desert, they said, "We are going to die in the desert." Who was the author of those words? Even though God made the promise multiple times, he could not get his people to agree with and speak his words.

Words are how you express your will and release your faith. For God to fulfill his promises, you have to release your faith and declare the promise. That promise has the seed to produce itself, and God has already blessed the place of its conception. Proverbs 18:21 states, "What you say can preserve life or destroy it; so you must accept the consequences of your words."

Now back to Abraham. Once God changed his name, what did he have to do? He had to notify his family and the hundreds of people who worked for him that his name was no longer Abram but Abraham. Now every time Abraham introduced himself, he heard father of many nations; every time Sarah said his name, she said father of many nations; every time one of his servants came to him with a question, they would say, "Father of many nations, what pasture do you want the sheep moved to?"

Every time that promise was spoken, it was producing the promise, father of many nations, because every promise carries the seed to produce itself. The Word of God literally produced a miracle in the body of both Abraham and Sarah, and their reproductive organs came to life, and then when they exercised their faith and came together, Isaac was born, and the rest is history.

A modern testimony

I heard a testimony from the late Bible teacher Derek Prince. In his twenties, he was drafted into the British Army during WWII and was sent to Northern Africa. While there, he contracted a skin infection that caused painful patches on his skin. The doctor prescribed a topical cream and told him to apply it to the affected areas three times a day, and it will clear up within seven to ten days. Weeks later, it was getting worse, so they sent him to a hospital. They determined it was viral so they prescribed antibiotics—one pill three times a day, for seven days, and it will clear up. Three weeks later, nothing had changed, and the doctors were searching for another course of action. One morning, he was reading his Bible, and he came to Proverbs 4:20–22 (NKJV), which says:

> My son, give attention to my words; Incline your ear to my sayings. Do not let them depart from your eyes; Keep them in the midst of your heart; For they are life to those who find them, And health to all their flesh.

The margin of his King James Bible said that the Hebrew word for health was *medicine*. Like a flash from heaven, the Holy Spirit revealed this truth to his heart as his answer. He decided that he would find the biblical promises that revealed healing, and he began to apply them to his heart three times a day. Verses like Psalm 107:20 (NKJV) says, "He sent His word and healed them, And delivered them from their destructions." First Peter 2:24 (NKJV) states, "Who Himself bore our sins in His own body on the tree, that we, having died to sins, might live for righteousness—by whose stripes you were healed." After thirty days of applying the medicine of God's Word to his heart, his skin was totally healed.

Here is the law of conception. Every promise of God carries the seed to produce itself, *and* God has blessed the place of your conception; therefore, all things are possible for those who believe.

Satan's deception: Convince us that God is the one controlling our destiny, all the while he is inundating us with words that produce destruction, then convincing us to blame God for his destruction.

Receiving by faith

We need to understand God's part is grace, and our part is faith. Ephesians 2:8–9 states:

> For by grace you have been saved through faith, and that not of yourselves; it is the gift of God, not of works, lest anyone should boast.

When we think of grace, we think unmerited favor, and that is true, but grace is such a big all-encompassing biblical truth. Grace describes everything that God has already done through the finished work of Christ to meet the total needs of man—spirit, soul, and body. Titus 2:11 says, "For the grace of God that brings salvation has appeared to all men."

We must understand that even though God's redemptive plan is finished, it is not received automatically by all people. Man has been given a free will, and God will never override the free will of man, even to accomplish his redemptive purposes.

Second Peter 3:9 states, "The Lord is not slack concerning His promise, as some count slackness, but is longsuffering toward us, not willing that any should perish but that all should come to repentance." God's plan is for everyone to come to repentance and be restored into relationship with him. Ask yourself, is everyone being saved? No, only those who choose to exercise their faith and receive this great gift.

Let me sum up faith like this: Faith is how you choose or exercise your free will, acting on what you believe. Faith is how God intended for you to receive what he has already provided by grace. Grace is God's part, salvation, and it is finished.

You got saved when you heard that Jesus had already made the payment for your sin. You believed that everyone who came to him got saved, and you exercised your faith by confessing with your mouth that he is Lord and that God raised him from the dead. Romans 10:9–10 states:

> That if you confess with your mouth the Lord Jesus and believe in your heart that God has raised Him from the dead, you will be saved. For with the heart one believes unto righteousness, and with the mouth confession is made unto salvation.

The same faith that you used to receive forgiveness of sin is the same faith you use to receive every benefit of God's great salvation.

A prophetic picture

The Exodus story is a prophetic picture of salvation.

- Egypt represents the kingdom of darkness, where God's people are kept in bondage.
- Pharaoh represents Satan, the one who keeps God's people in bondage.
- Moses represents Jesus, the one who delivers God's people from bondage.
- The promised land represents the kingdom of God, the place of abundance.

God made the promise to Abraham that his people would enter into Canaan. So the promise had already been provided; that was grace, God's part. The Israelites were to believe and act upon the promise; that was faith, their part.

In Hebrews 4, Paul brings great clarity as to why they didn't receive God's promise. Hebrews 4:2 (AMPC) states, "For indeed we have had the glad tidings [Gospel of God] proclaimed to us just as truly as they [the Israelites of old did when the good news of deliverance from bondage came to them]; but the message they heard did not benefit them, because it was not mixed with faith (with the leaning of the entire personality on God in absolute trust and confidence in His power, wisdom, and goodness) by those who heard it; neither were they united in faith with the ones [Joshua and Caleb] who heard (did believe)."

The good news or the Gospel is deliverance from the bondage of Satan. They did not receive the benefits of God's provision because they did not mix faith with the promise. Their faith was made ineffective because of who they believed. Joshua and Caleb revealed what faith looked like. They took God at his word and elevated his promises above their natural circumstances—the giants, armies, and fortified walls meant nothing to them because God's Word is true, so they said, "Let's go possess the land." The ten spies revealed what unbelief looks like. They elevated their natural circumstances, the giants, armies, and fortified walls above the promises of God, making the Word of God of no effect, and they chose not to enter in and possess the land, even though God had already provided it.

Please read Numbers 13. The children of Israel were right on the border of the promised land. It was theirs to possess. All they had to do was mix their faith with the promise, believe that God had already provided the promise, *and* step in, and possess the land.

The children of Israel did not miss out on the promise because God did not provide it, it was because they did not believe and act upon what God had already provided. This is what is happening to millions of people today. They are not receiving this great gift of salvation (healed, delivered, restored, and set free), not because it hasn't already been provided but because they are not mixing their faith with the promise, believing, and acting upon God's Word.

Let me sum up faith like this: Grace is what God has already provided, faith is how you choose or exercise your free will, acting on what you believe. Faith is how God intended for you to receive what he has already provided by grace. Grace is God's part, salvation, and it is finished.

Satan's strategy

Convince the church that God's plans happen automatically, that he decides if, when, where, and how we receive his promises, making his ways mysterious and our faith unnecessary.

CHAPTER 5

I Am a New Creation

Our error today is that we do not expect a converted man to be a transformed man, and as a result of this error our churches are full of substandard Christians. A revival is among other things a return to the belief that real faith invariably produces holiness of heart and righteousness of life.

—A. W. Tozer

Therefore, if anyone is in Christ, the new creation has come: The old has gone, the new is here!

—2 Corinthians 5:17

THIS WOULD INCLUDE our old identity, our life of sin, the power of Satan over you, the religious works of trying to please God, our old relationship with the world, and our old mindsets. We're not reformed or simply refurbished. We are made completely new by our union with Christ and the indwelling of the Holy Spirit (commentary notes: Passion Translation).

To know the truth, we have to understand God's original design.

Most people who study the human body teach that a human is a two-part being: the inner man (your spirit and soul combined) and your outer man, the body.

Many theologians have followed along the same line of thinking, but that is not what the Bible teaches.

In the Old Testament, in the first chapter of the Bible, God reveals his plan for man: create man in his image and likeness. Genesis 1:26 (NKJV) states, "Then God said, 'Let Us make man in Our image, according to Our likeness; let them have dominion over the fish of the sea, over the birds of the air, and over the cattle, over all the earth and over every creeping thing that creeps on the earth.'" Image describes man's ability to receive God's nature. Likeness describes man's ability to reveal God's nature.

When God made Adam in his image, he was referring to his spirit because God is a Spirit. Adam existed as a spirit being up until Genesis 2:7 (KJV), which says, "And the Lord God formed man of the dust of the ground, and breathed into his nostrils the breath of life; and man became a living soul." You can see from this scripture that now a body and soul have been added, and man had become a three-part being.

In the New Testament, a three-part being is also confirmed. "Now may the God of peace Himself sanctify you completely; and may your *whole spirit, soul, and body* [emphasis mine] be preserved blameless at the coming of our Lord Jesus Christ" (1 Thessalonians 5:23). The Bible teaches us that we are three-part beings—spirit, soul, and body.

This is also confirmed in Hebrews. "Because God's word is living, active, and sharper than any two-edged sword. It penetrates to the point that *it separates the soul from the spirit* [emphasis mine] and the joints from the marrow. It's able to judge the heart's thoughts and intentions" (Hebrews 4:12 CSB). If our spirit and soul were one thing, it could not be separated.

Your spirit is the core of your being, the real you. Your soul is your mind, will, and emotions. Your body is the physical part of you that can be seen and touched. *So, biblically speaking, you are a spirit being with a soul that lives in a body*!

As God's crown jewel of creation, those who bear his image, we are the only living beings that were designed to function in both of God's created realms: the spiritual realm and the natural realm of earth.

- Our spirits are designed to function in the spiritual realm, using our faith. Our spirit is how we hear from God, fellowship with God, receive, and reveal God's nature.
- Our soul (mind, will, and emotions) is how we function in the mental part of the natural realm, using logic and reason. This is how you learned math, science, and whatever skills you use to make a living.
- Our body is how we function in the material part of the natural world, using your five natural senses—taste, smell, feel, hear, and see. This is how you relate to other people and enjoy God's natural creation. You feel the warmth of an embrace, you smell the fragrance of a beautiful rose.

We must be very clear here about what God's image is. God declares that he is the source of life and light. God described his nature as love, joy, peace, patience, goodness, faithfulness, kindness, gentleness, and self-control. He also gave us his names, and they reveal his attributes. His names say that he is the source of our peace (Shalom), provision (Jireh), health (Rapha), victory (Nissi), righteousness (Tsidkenu), presence (Shamma), our guide (Shepherd).

When Adam sinned, his spirit was separated from the nature of God, and everything that God designed for men became *perverted* ("to turn from its proper purpose," *Webster's 1828 Dictionary*).

Here are the effects of spiritual separation.

Love became *self-centeredness*, joy became *sorrow*, peace became *stress*, patience became *impatience*, goodness became *evil*, faithfulness became *disloyalty*, kindness became *indifference*, gentleness became *harshness*, and self-control became *indulgence*, light became *darkness*, life became *death*, health became *sickness*, provision became *poverty*, presence became *separation*, victory became *defeat*, guidance became *deception*, and righteousness became *depravity*.

Please take time to look at every italized word and understand that none of these are God's design for you. Adam's nature was perverted through being separated from the nature of God, and that perverted nature was passed down to every human being through the bloodline of Adam.

Understanding our spiritual rebirth

As we have clearly seen, every human was born in Adam, and there was no way for us to get free from this perverted nature. The good news is that God had a plan to redeem us before the foundation of the world, and that plan was to send Jesus as our Redeemer. John 1:29 states, "The next day John saw Jesus coming toward him and said, 'Look, the Lamb of God, who takes away the sin of the world!'"

In the Old Testament, on the Day of Atonement, a spotless lamb was brought to the priest to be our sin substitute. The blood of that lamb had no power to atone for their sins. It was simply a type and shadow of Jesus.

Jesus came to be our substitute. For Jesus to be our substitute, he could not be born of the bloodline of Adam, so Joseph could not be his father. He was born of God through a miraculous virgin birth. Just like Adam in Genesis 1:27, Jesus was made in the image of God.

In the New Testament, there was a Day of Atonement. It was the day of Jesus's crucifixion. On that day, God's plan was to atone for everything that came through Adam.

Colossians 2:14 (TPT) states, "He canceled out every legal violation we had on our record and the old arrest warrant that stood to indict us. He erased it all—our sins, our stained soul—he deleted it all and they cannot be retrieved! *Everything we once were in Adam has been placed onto his cross and nailed permanently there as a public display of cancellation* [emphasis mine]."

To understand the truth about the atonement, please go back and write down every italized word that described what happened when Adam was separated from God's nature. Every one of those words were placed on Jesus's cross and canceled because they were never God's design for us. Then take time to meditate on these amazing biblical truths and begin to thank God for what he has done for you.

So we now see what God did with the nature of Adam. The question is how did he intend for us to be restored to his original design?

Galatians 2:20 (NKJV) says, "I have been crucified with Christ; it is no longer I who live, but Christ lives in me; and the life which I now live in the flesh I live by faith in the Son of God, who loved me and gave Himself for me."

You were born in Adam so when you got born again, your old nature was crucified with Christ and replaced with God's nature in Christ.

Second Corinthians 5:17 (NKJV) states, "Therefore, if anyone is in Christ, he is a new creation; old things have passed away; behold, all things have become new."

Now, to understand your new birth, go back and right down all of words that describe God's nature. Take the time to meditate on those amazing biblical truths and begin to thank him for who you are "in Christ."

Jesus confirms that it is our spirit that is born again.

"Nicodemus came to Jesus at night, inquiring about the kingdom that he had been preaching about and how one can enter into the kingdom, Jesus said this. Jesus answered and said to him, 'Most assuredly, I say to you, unless one is born again, he cannot see the kingdom of God'" (John 3:3).

Nicodemus, being a natural man, thought that Jesus was talking about a natural kingdom with a natural way to enter in. John 3:4 says, "Nicodemus said to Him, 'How can a man be born when he is old? Can he enter a second time into his mother's womb and be born?'"

Jesus immediately begins to contrast the difference between your natural birth and your new spiritual birth.

> Jesus answered, "Most assuredly, I say to you, unless one is born of water and the Spirit, he cannot enter the kingdom of God. That which is born of the flesh is flesh, and that which is born of the Spirit is spirit. Do not marvel that I said to you, 'You must be born again.' The wind blows where it wishes, and you hear the sound of it,

> but cannot tell where it comes from and where it goes. So is everyone who is born of the Spirit." (John 3:5–8)

Being born of water refers to your natural birth. When a mother's water breaks, the countdown begins, and soon a child is born. Then he continues his contrast by saying that which is born of the flesh is flesh, speaking of our natural birth.

That which is born of the Spirit is spirit refers to the spiritual rebirth. The new birth that Jesus was speaking about was the reconnection of man's spirit to God's Spirit or spiritual union.

Let's look at some of the scriptures that reveal this spiritual reunion.

- When Jesus began to talk about the coming of the Holy Spirit, he described how our spirits will become one with God in Christ Jesus. "At that day you will know that I am in My Father, and you in Me, and I in you" (John 14:20).
- Paul also describes this union. "But he who is joined to the Lord is one spirit with Him" (1 Corinthians 6:17).
- The author of Hebrews is the most clear. "For both he that sanctifieth [Jesus] and they who are sanctified [us] are all of one: for which cause he is not ashamed to call them brethren" (Hebrews 2:11 KJV). The phrase, "*are of one*," in the Greek means *one to the exclusion of another.*

The moment you are born again, your spirit and God's Spirit become one "*in Christ.*"

This is how Paul describes your born-again experience in the New Testament.

> For in Him the whole fullness of Deity (the Godhead) continues to dwell in bodily form [giving complete expression of the divine nature]. And you are in Him, made full and having come to fullness of life [in Christ you too are filled with

> the Godhead—Father, Son and Holy Spirit—and reach full spiritual stature]. And He is the Head of all rule and authority [of every angelic principality and power]. (Colossians 2:9–10 AMPC)

God put you "in Christ" so that you can receive the image or fullness of God.

God put Christ in you to reveal his nature and bring glory to him on the earth. "To them God willed to make known what are the riches of the glory of this mystery among the Gentiles: which is Christ in you, the hope of glory" (Colossians 1:27).

The Bible is a spiritual book revealing spiritual reality/truths. This is why every redemptive promise is presented as a past tense accomplishment. Jesus only atoned for your sin one time, and when you received the gift of salvation by faith, every benefit of the new birth became a reality in your born-again spirit.

Second Corinthians 1:20 (NLT) states, "For all of God's promises have been fulfilled in Christ with a resounding 'Yes!' And through Christ, our 'Amen' (which means 'Yes') ascends to God for his glory."

Second Peter 1:3 (TPT) says, "Everything we could ever need for life and godliness has already been deposited in us by his divine power. For all this was lavished upon us through the rich experience of knowing him who has called us by name and invited us to come to him through a glorious manifestation of his goodness."

Colossians 1:13 (NKJV) states, "He has delivered us from the power of darkness and conveyed us into the kingdom of the Son of His love."

Ephesians 1:3 (NKJV) says, "Blessed be the God and Father of our Lord Jesus Christ, who has blessed us with every spiritual blessing in the heavenly places in Christ."

First Peter 2:24 (NKJV) states, "Who Himself bore our sins in His own body on the tree, that we, having died to sins, might live for righteousness—by whose stripes you were healed."

Mind-blowing, right? If this is true, why am I not experiencing all of these benefits? I am glad you asked.

It is only your spirit that was born again. Your body was not born again.

I got saved in 1989. When I knelt down at the altar and prayed to receive Jesus, I was five-eleven, with a slender build and a fair complexion. When I got up from the altar as a new creation, my body was still the same because only my spirit was born again. If you were tall and slender before you got born again, you will be the same after.

Your soul (mind, will, and emotions) was not born again.

When I got up from that altar, my mind was still conformed to the patterns of this world. I still believed that all of the effects of sin were normal and to be expected, and my natural mind could only believe what I could see, taste, hear, smell, and feel.

Let's look at Paul's instructions in Romans 12:1–2, and it will bring some clarity to us.

> I beseech you therefore, brethren, by the mercies of God, that you present your bodies a living sacrifice, holy, acceptable to God, which is your reasonable service. And do not be conformed to this world, but be transformed by the renewing of your mind, that you may prove what is that good and acceptable and perfect will of God.

Paul encourages us to present our bodies as a living sacrifice or to submit our flesh unto God. If we can be honest, we have been led by the desires of the flesh our entire lives, and the Bible says that being led by the flesh leads to death. "If you live on the basis of selfishness, you are going to die. But if by the Spirit you put to death the actions of the body, you will live" (Romans 8:13 CEB).

Why does Paul encourage us to renew our minds if we are new creations? Because your soul was not made new, and we still have the same thought patterns that have created the wrong view of God, others, and ourselves.

One last exercise: take the list that you wrote down that describes the nature that came through Adam and compare them to the influences that our culture subjects us to. Most of the shows and commercials we watch, along with every form of media, are designed to convince us that this is your reality. You should expect to be sick, to have anxiety, to suffer lack, etc. These are the patterns of this world that Paul is saying have been conforming us.

Now remember that God designed you as a three-part being—spirit, soul, and body. Why did Paul only address two parts? Why did he only instruct us concerning our body and our mind (soul)? Because our spirit was already made perfect when we were joined to Christ.

How do we begin to release what is already true in our spirits so that we can live the abundant life that God planned for us?

I want to use two images to teach you this amazing truth.

I want to use this first illustration to help us understand how we were designed to function as human beings.

A Biblical Picture of Man

Man - A Three-Part Whole
(1 Thessalonians 5:23)

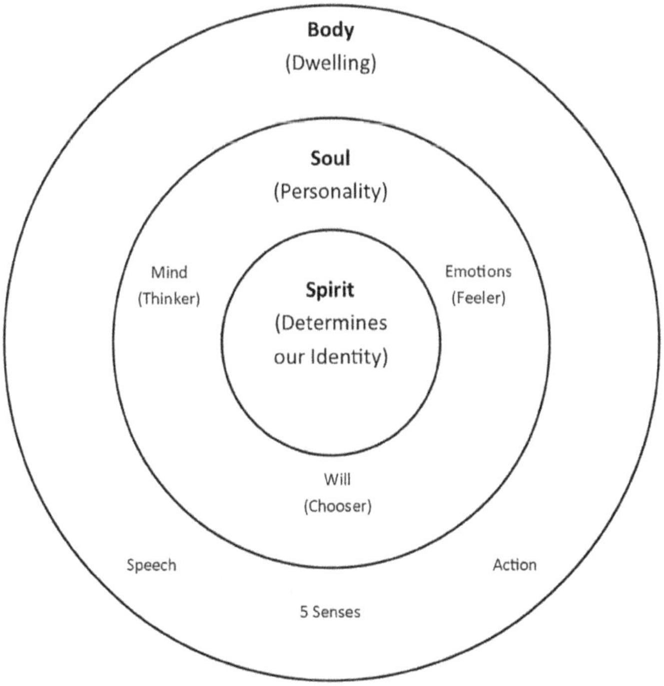

The inner circle represents your spirit, which is the real you. The middle circle represents your soul (mind, will, and emotions). The outer circle represents your physical body.

Your spirit has no direct connection with your physical body without flowing through your soul, the middle man.

Let me give you an example from the physical world. Think of your shower. You have a handle that is connected to a valve. If you want hot water, you turn the handle to hot, and it blocks the flow of cold water and releases the flow of hot water. The same thing is true if you want cold water. You simply turn the handle to cold, and it blocks the hot water and releases the cold. For most of us, we move the valve more toward the hot but still allow some cold water to flow so that we have warm water.

Spiritually speaking, your spirit is connected to God, who is the source of everything in the spiritual realm. Your body (flesh) only has access to the physical realm, which has been perverted by the effects of sin. Your soul or mind is the valve between the spirit and the body. If your mind is turned toward the spirit (in agreement with), believing the Word of God, spiritual realities are able to flow; if your mind is turned toward the flesh (filled with the patterns of this world and only operating with natural knowledge), it will block the flow of spiritual realities, and you will not experience what is already present in your spirit.

Your natural mind, which operates with natural knowledge and reason, have no capacity to believe the supernatural realities of the spirit. Your natural mind can only believe what it can see, taste, hear, smell, and feel; it literally rejects the supernatural realities of the spirit.

"Now the mind of the flesh [which is sense and reason without the Holy Spirit] is death [death that comprises all the miseries arising from sin, both here and hereafter]. But the mind of the [Holy] Spirit is life and [soul] peace [both now and forever]" (Romans 8:6 AMPC).

Your natural mind, unless transformed, will always be turned toward the flesh, releasing the deeds of the flesh that lead to death, and blocking the supernatural realities of the spirit or spiritual life.

The good news is that when your spirit was born again, it had the capacity, by faith, to believe the Word of God, in spite of your natural circumstances. Because God gave you a free will, he allows you to decide whether you want to operate in the flesh or the spirit.

When Paul talked about being transformed by the renewing of the mind, the word *transformed* in the Greek is *metamorphoō*. This is where we get the English word *metamorphoses*, which means to change the form or nature of a thing or person into a completely different onc. Picture a caterpillar spinning a cocoon and then coming out later as a beautiful butterfly.

When you choose to renew your mind to the Word of God, and you begin to operate in faith, it will come into an agreement with your spirit and release all of the supernatural spiritual realities that God has promised that lead to the life of God and block the flow of the flesh that leads to death.

When you choose to believe what is already true in your sprit, that you have received the fullness of God's nature, the fullness of his love, joy, peace, patience, goodness, kindness, gentleness, faithfulness, self-control, power, gifts, and anointing, and that your purpose in life is to reveal his nature to the world, then when you submit the desires of the flesh and renew your mind, you will begin to experience the holy calling and purpose that God envisioned for you before time began. "Who has saved us and called us with a holy calling, not according to our works, but according to His own purpose and grace which was given to us in Christ Jesus before time began" (2 Timothy 1:9).

Satan's strategy

Convince the church that we are forgiven but still have the nature that came through the fall of Adam.

CHAPTER 6

I Am Whole

WHOLENESS IS DEFINED as complete, sound, total well-being. God designed us to walk in wholeness physically, spiritually, and emotionally.

As I taught in the chapter on being a new creation, your spirit became complete the moment you were born again. Your spirit and God's Spirit became one. Your spirit is perfect and will never change for all of eternity.

Emotional wholeness

Every human was created with an innate desire to be accepted.

Acceptance is the action or process of being received as adequate or suitable, typically to be admitted into a group.

To understand acceptance, we have to answer two questions.

1) Who are we trying to be accepted by?
2) How do you become accepted?

In our culture, you find acceptance by how you look and what you do.

Remember all of the little clicks and groups in high school, the Barbie doll groups from the seventies with their petite bodies, poufy hair, and radiant skin? Or the cool cats of the fifties with their jeans, T-shirt, leather jackets, and their pompadour hairdos?

I have great news for you! Our God is extremely creative. Think about the diversity of plant and animal life. The same is true of the crown jewel of creation—mankind. There is great diversity among God's children, an endless array of shades of color, shapes, and sizes, and he is proud of them all. There are no weights and measures in heaven.

1) Who are we trying to be accepted by?

Our family, our peers, our coworkers, our social media group, our church.

Before I share my opinions about what I believe might be playing a role in the emotional conditions in our country, I want you to know that I am not a medical expert. I have not studied medical journals; heck, I didn't even consult Dr. Phil. These are simply observations based on my own life and raising five kids.

Our Founding Fathers looked to the Bible to find principles that would help govern a free society. They came up with a moral standard that, if followed, would allow each person to have a healthy, happy life, and treat others with dignity and respect.

Their hope was that each individual would submit their desires to these laws for their own good and the sake of others.

Over the last few decades, our culture has taught that there is no longer one standard for all people. Everyone has a right to choose their own standard to support their own lifestyle. Now we have all these different groups with all these different standards of truth, and conforming to their standard is what makes you acceptable to them. So you act a certain way around your family, but that is not acceptable to your peers, so on and so forth. Because you are trying to be so many things to so many people, and each group has their own standard of truth, you live in a state of constant emotional conflict. People do things with their peers that they deem acceptable, then they go back to their family, and because they have a different moral standard, they feel unaccepted by them, and the crazy cycle continues.

2) How do we become accepted?

We have to conform to the moral standards of each individual group. These moral standards are always changing, many times taking you further and further away from how your Creator designed you to live.

God's design for acceptance

God's design for us is to find acceptance in him alone because he is the source of unconditional love. God's nature is love, and he assigns value to people based on his nature, not their behavior.

What is acceptance according to God's Word?

Ephesians 1:3–6 says:

> Blessed be the God and Father of our Lord Jesus Christ, who has blessed us with every spiritual blessing in the heavenly places in Christ, just as He chose us in Him before the foundation of the world, that we should be holy and without blame before Him in love, having predestined us to adoption as sons by Jesus Christ to Himself, according to the good pleasure of His will, to the praise of the glory of His grace, by which *He made us accepted in the Beloved* [emphasis mine].

This word *accepted* is only used one other place in all of Scripture. "And having come in, the angel said to her, 'Rejoice, *highly favored* [emphasis mine] one, the Lord is with you; blessed are you among women!" (Luke 1:28). This is what the angel Gabriel said to Mary. The words *highly favored* are also translated *accepted* when God talks about you. Let that sink in. He used the same words to describe you and me that he used to describe the woman who would carry, give birth to, and raise the Son of God. *Wow*!

How does God say that we become accepted?

It was the perfect onetime sacrifice of Jesus for your sin that *made* you accepted. Hebrews 10:13 sates, "But this Man, after He had offered *one sacrifice for sins forever*, sat down at the right hand of God."

When we think of sin, we think of behavior, but that is the fruit of sin. What was put upon Jesus one time on the cross was the very *nature* of sin, the *root* that separated God and man in the garden. Once that sin payment was made, by faith, God and man can be reunited back to the oneness of God's design, and once that happens, nothing can separate you from God's love and acceptance. Romans 8:38–39 says:

> For I am persuaded that neither death nor life, nor angels nor principalities nor powers, nor things present nor things to come, nor height nor depth, nor any other created thing, shall be able to separate us from the love of God which is in Christ Jesus our Lord.

Here is how you walk in emotional wholeness. You believe in what Jesus has already done. You understand that it was the perfect sacrifice of Jesus that *made* you accepted. It was a grace gift, unmerited favor. If you didn't *do* anything to be made acceptable, nothing that you *do* can make you unacceptable.

Religion has taught many people that even after Jesus removed the nature of sin so we can be reunited with him in an eternal relationship, that what we *do* makes us unacceptable to God, and now there is something that you have to *do* to be accepted by God again. Some religions go as far as to teach that every time you sin, you lose your salvation and have to be born again and again and again. That is an exhausting lie straight from the pit of hell.

Let me cement this truth in your heart with a word picture. In the Old Testament, animal sacrifices were a prophetic picture of Jesus coming as our spotless Lamb to make a onetime sacrifice for our sin. Because the blood of animals could not forgive sin, it had to be done every year on the Day of Atonement. The sinner would find a lamb without spot or blemish and present it to the priest as an offering for his sin. Here is what I want you to get revelation of. Did the priest examine the sinner or the sacrifice? *The sacrifice. He examined the spotless lamb*!

Satan is the accuser of the brethren, so he will always try to point to your behavior and convince you that you are unacceptable before God. All you need to do is remind him that Jesus, the perfect Lamb, has already been sacrificed so that you could be made acceptable. Praise the Lord!

Physical wholeness

In Genesis, God said that everything he made was very good. Do you think that included cancer, Alzheimer's, or any other disease? No way. God never even intended for us to experience death, so what makes us think that sickness and disease were part of his plan?

When Adam sinned, man became separated from the source of life, and death entered into the human experience. Sickness is simply incipient death or the beginning stages of death. When Adam sinned, God's perfect design for man was perverted, and Adam's perfect blood became perverted. From that point on, sickness, disease, and deformity began to be passed down through the bloodline of Adam.

God made a covenant that he would bring healing to mankind. Exodus 15:26 states, "If you diligently heed the voice of the Lord your God and do what is right in His sight, give ear to His commandments and keep all His statutes, I will put none of the diseases on you which I have brought on the Egyptians. *For I am the Lord who heals you* [emphasis mine]."

Many scholars consider this the Old Testament healing covenant. This covenant was made absolutely certain when God joined his mighty name to the promise, calling himself Jehovah Rapha, the God who heals you. God's names reveal his attributes. Here his name reveals it is his nature to be the Healer, to recover to health, and sustain in health.

- Exodus 23:25 says, "So you shall serve the Lord your God, and He will bless your bread and your water. And *I will take sickness away from the midst of you* [emphasis mine]."

- Psalm 91:9–10 states, "Because you have made the Lord, who is my refuge, Even the Most High, your dwelling place, No evil shall befall you, *Nor shall any plague come near your dwelling* [emphasis mine]."
- Psalm 103:1–4 states, "Bless the Lord, O my soul; And all that is within me, bless His holy name! Bless the Lord, O my soul, And forget not all His benefits: Who forgives all your iniquities, *Who heals all your diseases* [emphasis mine]."
- Isaiah 53:4–5 says, "Surely He has borne our griefs [a]. And carried our sorrows [b]; Yet we esteemed Him stricken, Smitten by God, and afflicted. But He was wounded for our transgressions, He was bruised for our iniquities; The chastisement for our peace was upon Him, And *by His stripes we are healed* [emphasis mine]."
- Isaiah 53:11 states, "He shall see the labor of His soul, and be satisfied. By His knowledge My righteous Servant shall justify many, For He shall bear their iniquities."

The truth is that the Isaiah passages clearly teach that bodily healing is part of Christ's atoning work on the cross. The words *griefs* and *sorrows* specifically mean physical afflictions; furthermore, the words *borne*, *carried*, and *bear* are used to describe Jesus taking away the nature of sin (iniquities) in verse 11, and the effects or fruit of sin, sickness, in verse 4.

In spite of this clear teaching on the atonement, for centuries, some scholars have taught that the words *griefs* and *sorrows* are referring to spiritual affliction, and only spiritual healing is covered in the atonement.

Let me share what the Hebrew words are according to Bible Gateway Hebrew commentary.

- The literal Hebrew translation for griefs is [a] Isaiah 53:4; Lit. sickness.
- The literal Hebrew translation for sorrows is [b] Isaiah 53:4; Lit. pains.

One of the greatest ways to interpret the Scriptures is to allow them to speak for themselves.

Let's go to Matthew 8:16–17, where this verse is quoted, and it says:

> When evening had come, they brought to Him many who were demon-possessed. And He cast out the spirits with a word, *and healed all who were sick* [emphasis mine], that it might be fulfilled which was spoken by Isaiah the prophet, saying: "He Himself took our infirmities And bore our sicknesses."

In Matthew 8, Jesus physically healed the leper, healed enough people to cause the centurion to believe that if Jesus simply said the words, "Be healed," his servant would be healed of a physical affliction. Then Jesus healed Peter's mother-in-law of a severe fever (physical affliction) and all of the people who were brought to him in Capernaum that evening. *Yet, somehow, we still want to debate if healing was in the atonement.*

Root and fruit

Suppose that you had a beautiful apple tree in your yard, and the apples made the best pies that anyone had ever tasted. Everyone would always tell you that they wished they had a tree like that in their yard. Your neighbor was so jealous of your tree that he decided that if he couldn't have it, no one should, so while you were gone, he used his tractor to rip up your tree by the roots. What would happen to the fruit once the roots were removed? The fruit would die. Why? Because the source of their life is in the roots.

The nature of sin is the *root* of all of the effects of the fall. The fruit or effects of sin are sickness, disease, anger, wrath, malice, impatience, pride, lust, guilt, condemnation, shame, the list goes on and on.

Go back and read Psalm 103:1–4, and you will see that God forgave our sin (root) and healed our diseases (fruit). In Isaiah 53:4–5, he took away our sin (root) and took away our sickness (fruit).

Jesus deals with the root and the fruit.

Mark 2:1–12 says:

> And again He entered Capernaum after some days, and it was heard that He was in the house. Immediately many gathered together, so that there was no longer room to receive them, not even near the door. And He preached the word to them. Then they came to Him, bringing a paralytic who was carried by four men. And when they could not come near Him because of the crowd, they uncovered the roof where He was. So when they had broken through, they let down the bed on which the paralytic was lying. When Jesus saw their faith, He said to the paralytic, "*Son, your sins are forgiven you* [emphasis mine]." And some of the scribes were sitting there and reasoning in their hearts, "Why does this Man speak blasphemies like this? Who can forgive sins but God alone?" But immediately, when Jesus perceived in His spirit that they reasoned thus within themselves, He said to them, "Why do you reason about these things in your hearts? *Which is easier, to say to the paralytic, 'Your sins are forgiven you,' or to say, 'Arise, take up your bed and walk'? But that you may know that the Son of Man has power on earth to forgive sins"—He said to the paralytic, "I say to you, arise, take up your bed, and go to your house* [emphasis mine]." Immediately he arose, took up the bed, and went out in the presence of them all, so that all were amazed and glorified God, saying, "We never saw anything like this!"

This is a very familiar story. Many times, our familiarity keeps us from seeing the deeper truth that Jesus is teaching. This paralyzed man came for one reason: to be healed. Yet when Jesus addressed him, he said, "Your sins are forgiven." Was Jesus confused? Did he not know why he came? Jesus knew exactly what the man needed. The first thing that Jesus would have seen, when this man was lowered through the roof, was his paralyzed legs. If that was not enough, logic would have told him that if he could walk, he would have come through the door.

Pay close attention to what Jesus says to the scribes. "What is easier to say? Your sins are forgiven or rise up and walk?" What is Jesus trying to reveal to us? If you deal with the *root* of *sin*, the *fruit* of sin, sickness will be dealt with.

So to prove to these skeptics that Jesus had authority to forgive sin (root), he healed the sickness (fruit).

This is the same revelation that Jesus is teaching through communion.

When Jesus serves the Lord's Supper to his disciples, he is just days away from the cross. Jesus was part of the redemptive plan before the foundation of the world. He knew exactly what Isaiah 53 was prophesying. He knew that on the cross, his blood would be shed to remove the root or nature of sin, and his body would be beaten to remove the fruit of sin, sickness. So when he served the wine (his blood), it represented having the root of sin removed, and when he served the bread (his body), it represented having the fruit of sin, sickness, removed.

Further evidence

- Jesus came to reveal the Father's nature.

Hebrews 1:3a states, "He is the sole expression of the glory of God [the Light-being, the out-raying or radiance of the divine], and He is the perfect imprint and very image of [God's] nature."

John 14:9 says, "Jesus said to him, 'Have I been with you so long, and yet you have not known Me, Philip? He who has seen Me has seen the Father; so how can you say, "Show us the Father"?'"

- Jesus revealed God's nature to heal.

Matthew 14:23–24 states:

> Jesus ministered from place to place throughout all of the province of Galilee. He taught in the synagogues, preaching the wonderful news of the kingdom and healing every kind of sickness and disease among the people. His fame spread throughout all Syria! Many people who were in pain and suffering with every kind of illness were brought to Jesus for their healing—epileptics, paralytics, and those tormented by demonic powers were all set free. Everyone who was brought to Jesus was healed!

Jesus healed every sickness and every disease, and everyone who came to him got healed.

If even one person who came to Jesus did not get healed, he could not have said he came to reveal his Father's nature because the Father never changes.

- Jesus revealed God's nature of goodness by healing the sick.

Acts 10:38 states, "How God anointed Jesus of Nazareth with the Holy Spirit and with power, who went about doing good and healing all who were oppressed by the devil, for God was with Him."

- Jesus revealed God's nature to be merciful by healing the sick.

Matthew 15:22 says, "And behold, a woman of Canaan came from that region and cried out to Him, saying, 'Have mercy on me, O Lord, Son of David! My daughter is severely demon-possessed.'"

Matthew 5:28 states, "Then Jesus answered and said to her, 'O woman, great is your faith! Let it be to you as you desire.' And her daughter was healed from that very hour."

- Jesus revealed God's nature of compassion by healing the sick.

Matthew 20:32–34 says:

> So Jesus stood still and called them, and said, "What do you want Me to do for you?" They said to Him, "Lord, that our eyes may be opened." So Jesus had compassion and touched their eyes. And immediately their eyes received sight, and they followed Him.

- Jesus came to reveal the Father's will.

John 6:38 sates, "For I have come down from heaven, not to do My own will, but the will of Him who sent Me."

Luke 5:12–13 says:

> And it happened when He was in a certain city, that behold, a man who was full of leprosy saw Jesus; and he fell on his face and implored Him, saying, "Lord, if You are willing, You can make me clean." Then He put out His hand and touched him, saying, "I am willing; be cleansed." Immediately the leprosy left him.

The leper was saying, "I know you are able, but I am not sure you are willing." Why was he sure that Jesus was able? He heard that

Jesus healed every sickness and disease, and he knew that leprosy was included in *every*.

Why did the leper question Jesus's willingness? Some religious leaders taught that leprosy was God's judgment against sin. Could you imagine thinking that God made you sick and then trying to believe that it is his will to heal you?

There was only one answer for Jesus, "*I will!*" He could only do the will of the Father. John 6:38 testifies to this truth, and it states, "For I came down from heaven, not to do mine own will, but the will of him that sent me." The Father's will had already been established through an eternal covenant of healing and health, to recover to health, and to sustain in health. When Jesus went to the cross, he knew that his Father was going to put sin and sickness upon him so that it could be taken away from us and restore us back to his original design and intent.

When individuals came to Jesus to be healed, he would speak about their belief and faith. Matthew 9:27–29 says:

> When Jesus departed from there, two blind men followed Him, crying out and saying, "Son of David, have mercy on us!" And when He had come into the house, the blind men came to Him. And Jesus said to them, "Do you *believe* [emphasis mine] that I am able to do this?" They said to Him, "Yes, Lord." Then He touched their eyes, saying, "According to *your faith* [emphasis mine] let it be to you."

Belief is taking God at his word. Faith is acting on what you believe.

Let's look at how simple belief and faith was in the New Testament.

Jesus healed every sickness and disease, and everyone who came to Jesus was healed. Here was their belief: they heard that everyone who came to him got healed. Here was their faith: they came expecting to receive.

Compare this to your salvation experience. Your belief: you heard that Jesus was the Savior, and that everyone who came to him got saved. Your faith: you came expecting to receive.

God took away our sin (the root) and our sickness (the fruit) through one act of atonement, and he wants us to receive Jesus as our Healer, the same way that we received him as our Savior.

Satan's strategy

Convince the church that healing was not paid for through the atonement. No one ever questions God's will to save people because the payment was already made, and all you have to do is believe and receive. You can't question God's will for something he has already done, right? Because we don't have the same revelation of God's payment for our healing, most Christians believe that God is able to heal, but they are not sure that he is willing, so we pray, "If it be your will." That is a prayer of doubt.

Look at what the Bible says about doubt. James 1:6–8 states:

> But let him ask in faith, with no doubting, for he who doubts is like a wave of the sea driven and tossed by the wind. For let not that man suppose that he will receive anything from the Lord; he is a double-minded man, unstable in all his ways.

These words are not meant to bring judgment or condemnation to you but to guide you to the truth. It is the truth that sets you free. Our freedom in Christ is freedom from everything that was brought into our lives because of the fall of man. This includes anything that steals, kills, or destroys!

CHAPTER 7

I Am a Man of Authority

Man cannot do anything on earth without God and God will not do anything on earth without man's involvement.

—John Wesley

In the beginning, God revealed his plan for man. Genesis 1:26 (TLB) says, "Then God said, "Let us make a man—someone like ourselves, to be the master of all life upon the earth and in the skies and in the seas." God's plan was that man would be master over the earth. Psalm 115:16 (CEV) states, "The Lord has kept the heavens for himself, but he has given the earth to us humans."

God is sovereign, which means all-powerful, first in rank. He is the Creator and sustainer of the earth, yet in his plan was that he would work in divine partnership with man to accomplish his plans for the earth. Psalm 8:4–6 (TPT) says:

> Why would you bother with puny, mortal man or care about human beings? Yet what honor you have given to men, created only a little lower than Elohim, crowned with glory and magnificence. You have delegated to them rulership over all you have made, with everything under their authority, placing earth itself under the feet of your image-bearers.

How does authority work? Genesis 1:27–28 (NKJV) states:

> So God created man in His own image; in the image of God He created him; male and female He created them. Then God blessed them, and God said to them, "Be fruitful and multiply; fill the earth and subdue it; have dominion over the fish of the sea, over the birds of the air, and over every living thing that moves on the earth."

Dominion means to master or rule, to exercise authority. Authority is delegated power.

Think of a law enforcement officer. If you break the law, and his enforcement of that law includes arresting you, and he tells you to put your hands behind your head, the power of enforcement is not based on his physical stature. His badge gives him authority or the delegated power of the state that he represents.

As we will see, moving forward, the evidence presented in Scripture reveals the primary *way that God fulfills his plans on the earth is through divine partnership with his image bearer.*

First we have to understand how God released his power. Hebrews 11:3(TPT) says, "Faith empowers us to see that the universe was created and beautifully coordinated by the power of God's words! *He spoke* [emphasis mine] and the invisible realm gave birth to all that is seen." Everything that God created came from the power of his spoken Word, just read Genesis 1. The pattern you see is that God said, it became.

God didn't just create everything with the power of his words. He holds the world together with the power of his word. Hebrews 1:3 (CEV) states, "God's Son has all the brightness of God's own glory and is like him in every way. *By his own mighty word, he holds the universe together* [emphasis mine]. After the Son had washed away our sins, he sat down at the right side of the glorious God in heaven."

God said, one time, "Let there be light," and until he says otherwise, we will have light. Amen.

If God uses words to release his power, and God gave man authority to use his power, how did God intend man to release his power? Words.

The power of God's Word has not diminished one iota since he declared light be, but what has diminished is man's belief in the power of God's Word and a lack of understanding as to our role in fulfilling God's plans.

What we see here in the book of Exodus is God's plan to accomplish his will on the earth. He made a covenant with man called divine partnership.

When God heard the cries of his people in Egypt, he did not work alone. He found Moses to be his divine partner. Exodus 3:7–12 states:

> And the Lord said: "I have surely seen the oppression of My people who are in Egypt, and have heard their cry because of their taskmasters, for I know their sorrows. So I have come down to deliver them out of the hand of the Egyptians, and to bring them up from that land to a good and large land, to a land flowing with milk and honey, to the place of the Canaanites and the Hittites and the Amorites and the Perizzites and the Hivites and the Jebusites. Now therefore, behold, the cry of the children of Israel has come to Me, and I have also seen the oppression with which the Egyptians oppress them. Come now, therefore, and I will send you to Pharaoh that you may bring My people, the children of Israel, out of Egypt." But Moses said to God, "Who am I that I should go to Pharaoh, and that I should bring the children of Israel out of Egypt?" So He said, "I will certainly be with you. And this shall be a sign to you that I have sent you: When you have brought the people out of Egypt, you shall serve God on this mountain."

God said that he had seen the oppression of his people, and he came down to deliver them, so he recruits Moses to go on his behalf. He needs a physical representation, yet he says that he will be the source of power. When Moses asks, "Who am I to go?" God didn't tell Moses how awesome he was or that he had the ability to accomplish the task. He simply said, "I will be with you."

God prepares Moses for his first meeting with Pharaoh: Exodus 7:1–2 says:

> So the Lord said to Moses: "See, I have made you as God to Pharaoh, and Aaron your brother shall be your prophet. You shall speak all that I command you. And Aaron your brother shall tell Pharaoh to send the children of Israel out of his land."

Is God telling Moses that he is making him the fourth member of the Godhead? No way. He is saying that he is going to work through Moses's words in a way that will make Pharaoh think that Moses is like God.

Please take the time to read the story of the ten plagues before you continue. I promise you will see a pattern you never saw before. Whatever God wanted to accomplish, he spoke to Moses, then when Moses spoke what God said to say or did what God said to do, then and only then was the power of God released to accomplish the assignment.

Here in Psalm 105, King David is retelling the exodus story. Pay close attention to his words. Psalm 105:26–28 states:

> But he sent them his faithful servant, Moses, the deliverer and chose Aaron to accompany him. *Their command* [emphasis mine] brought down signs and wonders, working miracles in Egypt. *By God's direction, they spoke and released a plague of thick darkness over the land* [emphasis mine].

The signs and wonders were released through Moses and Aaron's command. God directed them, and when they obeyed and spoke, the power of God was released.

I know that this is mind-blowing because we have been taught that sovereignty means God controls and does everything and man has no part. When you understand that *you* are in partnership with God, you will never see the Bible the same way again. God did not speak directly to the wall of Jericho or the Jordan River; he directed Joshua, and when he obeyed, the power of God was released.

Let me quickly sum up God's plan for us: God directs, man obeys, God releases his power to fulfill the promise.

Here's another example of divine partnership. After the Israelites crossed the Red Sea, Pharaoh came after them, and they were trapped. They had an army on one side, and the Red Sea on the other. Moses gave this great speech about how God would deliver them. Moses seemed to have had a momentary lapse into fear and must have cried out to God for help, forgetting the covenant of divine partnership. Exodus 14:15–16 states:

> And the Lord said to Moses, "*Why do you cry to Me* [emphasis mine]? Tell the children of Israel to go forward. *But lift up your rod, and stretch out your hand over the sea and divide it* [emphasis mine]. And the children of Israel shall go on dry ground through the midst of the sea.

God instructed Moses, Moses obeyed, God released his power to fulfill the assignment.

Authority continues in the New Testament

How Jesus accomplished God's plan. Philippians 2:7 says, "But emptied Himself [without renouncing or diminishing His deity, but only temporarily giving up the outward expression of divine equality and His rightful dignity] by assuming the form of a bond-servant, and being made in the likeness of men [He became completely human but was without sin, being fully God and fully man]." Jesus was 100 percent God and man. He never ceased to be God, yet he chose to set aside his divinity and operate as a man.

Jesus had to operate as a man because a perfect man had to restore what was lost by a man. And God had given authority to man on the earth.

John 14:10–11 states:

> Don't you believe that the Father is living in me and that I am living in the Father? Even my words are not my own but come from my Father, for he lives in me and performs his miracles of power through me. Believe that I live as one with my Father and that my Father lives as one with me—or at least, believe because of the mighty miracles I have done.

Jesus is saying that it is the Father working through him to accomplish his purposes.

How did Jesus fulfill the Father's will on the earth? He heard from the Father, he did what the Father said to do, and the Father released his power to perform the assignment.

A revelation of Jesus's authority is found in the book of Matthew. Matthew 8:6–9 says:

> When Jesus arrived in Capernaum, a Roman army captain came and pled with him to come to his home and heal his servant boy who was in bed paralyzed and racked with pain. "Yes," Jesus said, "I will come and heal him." Then the officer said, "Sir, I am not worthy to have you in my home; and it isn't necessary for you to come. If you will only stand here and say, 'Be healed,' my servant will get well! I know, because I am under the authority of my superior officers and I have authority over my soldiers, and I say to one,

> 'Go,' and he goes, and to another, 'Come,' and he comes, and to my slave boy, 'Do this or that,' and he does it. And I know you have authority to tell his sickness to go—and it will go!"

The centurion was a Roman officer who was in charge of a hundred men. At this point, the whole area of Palestine was under Roman occupation, and the centurion's job was to keep the peace. The greatest threat to peace would be large crowds. If a large crowd got stirred up, they could cause a riot, and that was unacceptable.

This centurion was assigned to the region of Galilee, where there happened to be a man named Jesus that was drawing great multitudes of people. Because the centurion was responsible for keeping the peace, it is likely that he would position himself near the person who was addressing the crowd.

What did he witness as he watched Jesus? We can imagine that he saw Jesus speak to blind eyes, deaf ears, paralyzed bodies, and he watched every one of them get healed. He probably also watched Jesus cast out demons with the power of his words.

What was his conclusion to Jesus's ministry? That Jesus had authority to use the power of someone greater than himself.

As a Roman officer, he was familiar with authority. For them, Caesar was their god, and when Caesar spoke, whatever he said came to pass. He spoke to his generals, and they did whatever was necessary to see it accomplished. They passed it on to the centurions, and they followed the command. The centurions gave the command to their subordinates, and they obeyed, all because of the authority of Caesar.

What did Jesus call the greatest faith? The person who understood the power of Jesus's words. "Just stand here and say, 'Be healed, and my servant will be healed.'" He understood that Jesus was exercising the authority that was from a source greater than himself. "I know you have authority to tell this sickness to go, and it will go."

Jesus passes on his authority

First Jesus gives his twelve apostles authority and commissions them to preach the Gospel and demonstrate that the kingdom has arrived. Luke 9:1–2 (TPT) states:

> Jesus summoned together his twelve apostles and imparted to them *authority* [emphasis mine] over every demon and the *power* [emphasis mine] to heal every disease. Then he commissioned them to proclaim God's kingdom and to heal the sick to *demonstrate* [emphasis mine] that the kingdom had arrived.

Then seventy other believers are given authority and commissioned to preach and demonstrate the kingdom. Luke 10:1 says, "After these things the Lord appointed seventy others also, and sent them two by two before His face into every city and place where He Himself was about to go." Luke 10:9 states, "And heal the sick there, and say to them, 'The kingdom of God has come near to you.'"

Jesus gives authority to the church and commissions us to preach and demonstrate the kingdom. John 14:12–14 (TPT) says:

> I tell you this timeless truth: The person who follows me in faith, believing in me, will do the same mighty miracles that I do—even greater miracles than these because I go to be with my Father! For I will do whatever you ask me to do when you ask me in my name. And that is how the Son will show what the Father is really like and bring glory to him. Ask me anything in my name, and I will do it for you!

To understand what Jesus is teaching, we have to understand the context of his conversation. Refer back to John 14:10–11. Jesus was telling his disciples how he was doing the works that were revealing the Father's nature and glorifying him by destroying the works of the devil and demonstrating that the kingdom had arrived. First John 3:8b states, "For this purpose the Son of God was manifested, that He might destroy the works of the devil."

In John 14:12, Jesus begins to teach the church how we are going to use authority to continue his ministry on the earth after he leaves.

First we have to understand how Jesus is using the word *ask* here. According to *Strong's Concordance*, the word *ask* can mean to request, demand, or desire.

Let me remind you that the purpose of our authority is to reveal the Father's nature so that he is glorified and to continue his work on the earth of furthering his kingdom.

Jesus is saying if you want to reveal the Father's nature and further his kingdom by destroying the works of the devil, you have to do it through *commanding the works of the devil* to leave in the power of his name.

Luke 10:17 (TPT) states, "When the seventy missionaries returned to Jesus, they were ecstatic with joy, telling him, 'Lord, even the demons obeyed us when *we commanded them in your name* [emphasis mine]!'"

The power of the name of Jesus

Ephesians 1:21 (NKJV) says, "Far above all principality and power and might and dominion, and every name that is named, not only in this age but also in that which is to come."

Philippians 2:9–11 (NKJV) states:

> Therefore God also has highly exalted Him and given Him the name which is above every name, that at the name of Jesus every knee should bow, of those in heaven, and of those on earth, and of those under the earth, and that every tongue should confess that Jesus Christ is Lord, to the glory of God the Father.

Every demonic assault that has come against mankind has a name, every disease has a name, every stronghold has a name. The name of Jesus has the power to destroy any name that comes against God's people.

The name of Jesus at work

Acts 3:6–8 states:

> Then Peter said, "Silver and gold I do not have, but what I do have I give you: *In the name of Jesus Christ of Nazareth, rise up and walk* [emphasis mine]." And he took him by the right hand and lifted him up, and immediately his feet and ankle bones received strength. So he, leaping up, stood and walked and entered the temple with them—walking, leaping, and praising God.

Thousands of people were in Jerusalem when this miracle happened, and they came to Peter and John to find out how it happened.

Acts 3:16 (TLB) says, "Jesus' name has healed this man—and you know how lame he was before. *Faith in Jesus' name* [emphasis mine]—faith given us from God—has caused this perfect healing."

The religious leaders could not hide the fact that this miracle had taken place, and five thousand men, plus women and children had already believed in Jesus and begun to follow the apostles, so they had to figure how to keep the message from spreading any further. They met, and they came up with this plan.

Acts 4:18 states, "So they called them and commanded them not to speak at all nor teach in the *name of Jesus* [emphasis mine]."

They understood that it was the combination of the preaching of the Word and the demonstration of the miracles that was attracting people to the church. They realized that if they could keep them from the power of Jesus's name, then they would have a message but no miraculous demonstration to attract the people.

The Great Commission

Mark 16:15–18 says:

> And He said to them, "Go into all the world and preach the gospel to every creature. He who believes and is baptized will be saved; but he who does not believe will be condemned. And these signs will follow those who believe: *In My name* [emphasis mine] they will cast out demons; they will speak with new tongues; they will take up serpents; and if they drink anything deadly, it will by no means hurt them; they will lay hands on the sick, and they will recover."

Jesus is speaking to his eleven disciples, and he is giving the same commission that he had given before. Preach the Gospel and heal the sick to demonstrate that the kingdom has arrived. In verse 17, Jesus is talking to everyone who would one day follow the disciples, which includes all of us, and he gives us the same command and the same source of power.

Maybe you are thinking that this is not even the Great Commission. That's because we are only familiar with Matthew's version of it.

Matthew 28:18–20 states:

> And Jesus came and spoke to them, saying, "All authority has been given to Me in heaven and on earth. Go therefore and make disciples of all the nations, baptizing them in the name of the Father and of the Son and of the Holy Spirit, teaching them to observe all things that I have commanded you; and lo, I am with you always, even to the end of the age."

Amen.

Matthew did not give as much detail as Mark did, he simply said, "Teach them to observe all things I commanded you."

Let's look at what Jesus commanded them to do and see if the message is consistent. Matthew 10:5–8 says:

> These twelve Jesus sent out and commanded them, saying: "Do not go into the way of the Gentiles, and do not enter a city of the Samaritans. But go rather to the lost sheep of the house of Israel. And as you go, preach, saying, '*The kingdom of heaven is at hand.' Heal the sick, cleanse the lepers, raise the dead, cast out demons. Freely you have received, freely give* [emphasis mine]."

The Bible is very clear that the Gospel should be seen and heard. There should be miracles to validate the gospel message.

- Hebrews 2:3–4 states, "How shall we escape if we neglect so great a salvation, which at the first began to be spoken by the Lord, and was confirmed to us by those who heard Him, *God also bearing witness both with signs and wonders, with various miracles, and gifts of the Holy Spirit, according to His own will* [emphasis mine]?"
- Mark 16:19–20 says, "So then, after the Lord had spoken to them, He was received up into heaven, and sat down at the right hand of God. And they went out and preached everywhere, *the Lord working with them and confirming the word through the accompanying signs* [emphasis mine]. Amen."

Miracles are not only how God intended to reveal his nature and plan to the earth, but they were also the signs that led people to the church. Maybe the reason that people are not finding their way to the church today is because we stopped using the signs that were intended to lead them there.

Satan's strategy

Convince the church that God accomplishes his purposes without their cooperation, that we simply pray and wait for God to move. Jesus is the head of the church, and he calls the church his body. The role of the head is to give instructions. The role of the body is to carry them out.

"I am the vine, you are the branches. He who abides in Me, and I in him, bears much fruit; for without Me you can do nothing" (John 15:5 NKJV).

We understand that God is the source (the vine), and we are the branches, and without him we can't bear fruit. Ask yourself this, how can God's purposes of revealing his fruit be done without the branch?

CHAPTER 8

I Am Righteous

> Christ took our sins and the sins of the whole world as well as the Father's wrath on his shoulders, and he has drowned them both in himself so that we are thereby reconciled to God and become completely righteous.
>
> —Martin Luther

The Bible speaks about two types of righteousness.

1) Righteousness is right standing or a position of acceptance in the presence of God. This describes your vertical relationship between you and God, based solely on what Jesus did.
2) Righteousness is also the behavior or fruit of a transformed life. This describes how what Jesus did affects your behavior toward others or our horizontal relationships.

The vertical is based on what Jesus did, the horizontal is based on what we do because of what Jesus did.

Vertical

Vertical righteousness cannot be established by any form of human effort.

"Therefore, since we have been made right in God's sight by faith, we have peace with God because of what Jesus Christ our Lord has done for us. Because of our faith, Christ has brought us into this place of undeserved privilege where we now stand, and we confidently and joyfully look forward to sharing God's glory" (Romans 5:1–2 NLT).

It is our faith in the redemptive work of Jesus that puts us in the place of undeserved privilege.

"But no one earns God's righteousness. It can only be transferred when we no longer rely on our own works, but believe in the one who powerfully declares the ungodly to be righteous in his eyes. It is faith that transfers God's righteousness into your account" (Romans 4:5 TPT)!

This vertical righteousness is based solely on what Jesus did for us.

Second Corinthians 5:21 says, "For He made Him who knew no sin to be sin for us, that we might become the righteousness of God in Him."

This one verse is perhaps the greatest verse in the New Testament to describe our salvation through the sinless Savior and his substitutionary death on the cross. A wonderful exchange took place on the cross. All of our sins were left there, our guilt was removed and forever gone, and we walked away with all of God's righteousness. What bliss is ours! Every believer today possesses the perfect and complete righteousness of Christ. We are seen by God as righteous as his Son.

Romans 5:19 states, "For as by one man's disobedience many were made sinners, so also by one Man's obedience many will be made righteous."

Sin is the barrier that separated God and man. There had to be a payment made for sin so that man could be restored back to right standing with God. This is what atonement means.

For sin to be atoned for, there had to be a perfect sacrifice. The Old Testament picture of this was when a sinner brought an offering for their sin. It had to be a lamb without spot or blemish.

This picture will set you free. When the sinner brought their sacrifice to the priest, did the priest examine the sinner or the sacrifice? It did not say that the person had to be without spot or blemish. It said the sacrifice had to be. Our right standing with God has nothing to do with our condition. It's the condition of the lamb.

John 1:29 states, "The next day John saw Jesus coming toward him, and said, "Behold! The Lamb of God who takes away the sin of the world!"

For us to have full confidence in our right standing, we have to take ourselves out of the equation and trust that the Lamb was a worthy sacrifice.

The virgin birth is the key to our confidence in Jesus's sacrifice. Luke 1:34–35 says:

> Then Mary said to the angel, "How can this be, since I do not know a man?" And the angel answered and said to her, "The Holy Spirit will come upon you, and the power of the Highest will overshadow you; therefore, also, that Holy One who is to be born will be called the Son of God."

Sin affected humanity at the DNA level. What was once perfect became imperfect, and that imperfection was passed down through the seed of Adam.

Jesus had to be born of a different seed to qualify as the perfect sacrifice, so he received the seed of God, not Adam.

When Satan wants to call your right standing into question, he gets you to examine yourself, your thoughts, your actions, your past, and not the perfect Lamb.

When Satan questions your righteousness, point him to the perfect Lamb.

Horizontal

Righteousness is also the behavior or fruit of a transformed life. Philippians 1:8–11 states:

> For God is my witness, how I yearn for you all with the affection of Christ Jesus. And it is my prayer that your love may abound more and more, with knowledge and all discernment, so

> that you may approve what is excellent, and so be pure and blameless for the day of Christ, filled with the fruit of righteousness that comes through Jesus Christ, to the glory and praise of God.

This describes how what Jesus did affects your behavior toward others or our horizontal relationships.

The fruit of horizontal relationship is love. Galatians 5:22–23 (TPT) states, "But the fruit produced by the Holy Spirit within you is divine love in all its varied expressions: joy that overflows, peace that subdues, patience that endures, kindness in action, a life full of virtue, faith that prevails, gentleness of heart, and strength of spirit. Never set the law above these qualities, for they are meant to be limitless."

Biblical love is *the* evidence that you are a follower of Jesus. John 13:34–35 says, "A new commandment I give to you, that you love one another; as I have loved you, that you also love one another. By this all will know that you are My disciples, if you have love for one another."

Biblical love puts the needs of others above its own. John 15:13 states, "Greater love has no one than this, than to lay down one's life for his friends."

Biblical love is *the* glue that holds all human relationships together.

Biblical love is based on a choice, not feelings.

Biblical love is a choice to value people apart from behavior.

When you were born again, in your spirit you received the fullness of God's unconditional love. All you have to do is choose to release it.

First Corinthians 13:4–7 (MSG) says:

> Love never gives up. Love cares more for others than for self. Love doesn't want what it doesn't have. Love doesn't strut, Doesn't have a swelled head, Doesn't force itself on others, Isn't always

> "me first," Doesn't fly off the handle, Doesn't keep score of the sins of others, Doesn't revel when others grovel, Takes pleasure in the flowering of truth, Puts up with anything, Trusts God always, Always looks for the best, Never looks back, But keeps going to the end.

Righteousness is one of the keys to victory. Not just in your own life, but the life of the church.

When you get established in the fact that right standing is based on Jesus, the spotless Lamb, and not your behavior, you will be able to abide in Jesus always, and the result is that you will bear kingdom fruit.

The vertical fruit of right standing will always produce the fruit of right living, and that will draw people to Christ.

It is the goodness of God that leads man to repentance.

Satan's strategy

Convince the church that righteousness means perfection based on our human effort, keeping us from coming boldly to the throne of grace.

CHAPTER 9

I Am Free

The freest I will ever be is when I am free of me.

—Jim Nave

As Americans, one of the things we value most is our freedom. Our country was built on the foundation of religious freedom. We were not going to allow men to dictate how or when we worship God.

Galatians 5 has become one of my favorite chapters in the Bible because Paul talks about freedom. He is not talking about freedom from Roman oppression. He is talking about freedom from spiritual oppression.

Let me be clear, the Anointed One has set us free—not partially, but completely and wonderfully free! "We must always cherish this truth and stubbornly refuse to go back into the bondage of our past" (Galatians 5:1 TPT). It is true! Because of the finished work of Christ, we are free! He warns us not to go back to the bondage of our past.

The apostle Paul tells us what freedom is and what the source of that freedom is. "Beloved ones, God has called us to live a life of freedom in the Holy Spirit. But don't view this wonderful freedom as an opportunity to set up a base of operations in the natural realm" (Galatians 5:13 TPT).

First he tells us where freedom is found—in the Holy Spirit. True freedom is when you are filled, led, and empowered by the Holy Spirit. "As you yield freely and fully to the dynamic life and power of the Holy Spirit, you will abandon the cravings of your self-life. For your self-life craves the things that offend the Holy Spirit and hinder him from living free within you! And the Holy Spirit's intense cravings hinder your old self-life from dominating you! So then, the two incompatible and conflicting forces within you are your self-life of the flesh and the new creation life of the Spirit" (Galatians 5:16–17).

What is the opposite of freedom? Bondage, right? What is the opposite of the spirit? The flesh.

Living to please ourselves is what hinders the work of the Holy Spirit in our lives. It is the bondage of our past that Paul addressed in Galatians 5:1. The strategy of the enemy is to tempt us to live outside of God's design and intent for our lives. As long as we live from the old man or the "self-man," we will always be subjectable to his temptation and schemes.

Let me use a fishing analogy to explain. A hook is part of the tool the enemy uses to pull the old man out of the grave. If you want to catch fish, you have to use more than a hook. You have to figure out what they are hungry for and entice them with it—bait. Our hunger is the cravings of the self-life, and that is the bait the enemy uses to entice us to live outside of our design or the new man.

He knows full well how to entice you because he has ruled you most of your life. He uses bait like fear, worry, low self-esteem, anger, lust, pride, jealousy, impatience, any form of self-centeredness will do. He uses these feelings to entice you into the very behaviors that are outside of God's design for you, and they are always harmful for you and others. Everything listed in the verses below are the fruit of his enticement because of self-centeredness.

Galatians 5:19–21 states:

> The cravings of the self-life are obvious: Sexual immorality, lustful thoughts, pornography, chasing after things instead of God, manipulating others, hatred of those who get in your way, senseless arguments, resentment when others are favored, temper tantrums, angry quarrels, only thinking of yourself, being in love with your own opinions, being envious of the blessings of

> others, murder, uncontrolled addictions, wild parties, and all other similar behavior. Haven't I already warned you that those who use their "freedom" for these things will not inherit the kingdom realm of God!

Freedom means that we become so completely free of self-indulgence that we become servants of one another, expressing love in all we do, for love completes the laws of God. "All of the law can be summarized in one grand statement: 'Demonstrate love to your neighbor, even as you care for and love yourself'" (Galatians 5:14 TPT).

God made man in his image, and his image is love, and the purpose of love is to give or prefer others above ourselves. Through the fall, we went from love to self-centeredness, from lovers who give to consumers who take.

Created to give

"This generous God who supplies abundant seed for the farmer, which becomes bread for our meals, is even more extravagant toward you. First he supplies every need, plus more. Then he multiplies the seed as you sow it, so that the harvest of your generosity will grow. You will be abundantly enriched in every way as you give generously on every occasion" (2 Corinthians 9:10–11 TPT).

God is the source off all things, and he always gives you enough seed for you and extra seed to be a blessing to others. You have a choice to either consume all of your seeds or sow some into the lives of others. It is only the seeds that you sow that God can multiply. Most of us only relate this to money, but this is how God intends to bring increase into your life. The answer to having your needs met is to sow a seed. If you need encouragement, sow encouragement; if you need love, sow a seed of love, and whatever you sow, God promises to increase.

My prayer

Father, thank you that you created me in your image, which is love. So, right now, I put off the selfish mindsets that keep me in bondage, things like impatience, unkindness, pride, the desire to put my needs above others, my inability to celebrate others' victories, and I put on love because love always prefers others above itself. Love always sees the best and expects the best. Love keeps no record of wrongs. Lord, today, I give up every right but to love you and others.

Satan's strategy

Convince the church that self-centeredness is normal so that he can continue to tempt us in the flesh, causing hurt and pain in the lives of those we love.

CHAPTER 10

I Am a Man of the Word and Spirit

> If you have the word without the Spirit you dry up! If you have the Spirit without the word you blow up but if you have the word and the Spirit you grow up.
>
> —Jack Taylor

ONE OF THE greatest strategies of the enemy is to divide and conquer! What a magnificent job he has done with the body of Christ. He has used the Word and the Spirit to bring great division when God's goal is unity.

There has been a divorce in the body of Christ, and just like in a natural divorce, the kids are split between parents. In the body of Christ, some kids went with the Word, some with the Spirit. This action has led to theological extremes, division, and judgment.

The danger is in extreme views

An extreme view of the Word.

The Word people focus on knowing about God. The basis of their experience is logic and intellect. Reading the Bible becomes a fact-finding journey. Their lives are founded on following principles and rules. They use fear as motivation to shape behavior. And worst of all, they reject or discount anything in Scripture they can't understand using human logic and reason. They say there is no need for the Spirit or his gifts, now that we have the Word. Their biggest fear is not having control.

An extreme view of the Spirit.

The Spirit people focus on knowing God, but the basis of their experience is feelings or experiences based on emotion or what you could call spiritual highs. They talk a lot about spending time with God, but reading the Word is not a big part of their time with him. Without the Word to guide them, everything is acceptable. They say we don't need the Word as a guide because the Spirit leads us. Their biggest fear is being controlled.

The Word.

The Word of God is infallible, which means incapable of error.

"We also have the prophetic message as something completely reliable, and you will do well to pay attention to it, as to a light shining in a dark place, until the day dawns and the morning star rises in your hearts" (2 Peter 1:19).

The Word of God is divinely inspired.

"All Scripture is God-breathed and is useful for teaching, rebuking, correcting and training in righteousness, so that the servant of God may be thoroughly equipped for every good work" (2 Timothy 3:16–17).

The Word of God is alive and active.

"For the word of God is alive and active. Sharper than any double-edged sword, it penetrates even to dividing soul and spirit, joints and marrow; it judges the thoughts and attitudes of the heart" (Hebrews 4:12).

The Bible is the bedrock of all of our thoughts and actions, the foundation of truth, and the cornerstone of our lives.

The Spirit.

The Holy Spirit is the divine interpreter, our spiritual guide, our divine empowerment for Christlike living, and the power necessary to accomplish our divine calling of making disciples of all the earth.

Divine interpreter.

First Corinthians 2:9–13 states:

> However, as it is written: "What no eye has seen, what no ear has heard, and what no human mind has conceived" the things God has prepared for

> those who love him— these are the things God has revealed to us by his Spirit. The Spirit searches all things, even the deep things of God. For who knows a person's thoughts except their own spirit within them? In the same way no one knows the thoughts of God except the Spirit of God. What we have received is not the spirit of the world, but the Spirit who is from God, so that we may understand what God has freely given us. This is what we speak, not in words taught us by human wisdom but in words taught by the Spirit, explaining spiritual realities with Spirit-taught words.

As great a gift as logic and intellect are, they are incapable of properly interpreting Scripture. According to the Word we believe to be divinely inspired, Scripture can only be revealed by the Spirit.

Our divine guide.

"I have much more to say to you, more than you can now bear. But when he, the Spirit of truth, comes, he will guide you into all the truth. He will not speak on his own; he will speak only what he hears, and he will tell you what is yet to come" (John 16:12–13).

Think about the role of a guide. Have you ever taken a guided tour? They bring the details beyond what you can get by just following the tourist signs. They know the truth beyond the folklore.

Our quest as we approach the Scripture must always be truth. We have to allow truth to be the standard for everything. Truth will always line up with the nature of God. Truth has to dictate our experience, not the other way around. When we allow our experience to shape truth, we create doctrines that are not consistent with the nature of God.

The promise of the Father.

The Father promised that he would send the Holy Spirit. The purpose was to restore what was lost in the fall, our identity and purpose.

Let's start first with identity. Some of the confusion is because he uses the same phrase to describe both works of the Spirit being in you or filled with the Spirit and empowered by the Spirit.

Filled with the Spirit.

There is much controversy regarding the role of the Holy Spirit in the lives of believers. For some, he is imperative to their Christian walk. Some minimize his role, and some ignore him completely and are satisfied doing life and ministry in their own power.

The promise to restore our identity.

When Jesus tells of the coming of the Spirit, he says he will be in (filling) you.

John 14:15–17 states:

> If you love me, keep my commands. And I will ask the Father, and he will give you another advocate to help you and be with you forever—the Spirit of truth. The world cannot accept him, because it neither sees him nor knows him. But you know him, for he lives with you and will be in you.

There are many words used to describe the Holy Spirit: *fire, wind, oil, water.*

In John 4, Jesus is talking to the Samaritan woman about salvation, and he uses water to describe what happens. "But whoever drinks the water I give them will never thirst. Indeed, the water I give them will become in them a spring of water welling up to eternal life" (John 4:14).

Jesus is saying that when you are saved, the Holy Spirit will well up inside you. He is describing becoming a new creation. The Holy Spirit is the tangible substance of God or the nature of God. The blood of Jesus cleanses you, and now you receive your new nature or are restored back to your original design. "Therefore, if anyone is in Christ, the new creation has come: The old has gone, the new is here!" (2 Corinthians 5:17).

> Paul is saying that you have been made complete (given a new nature). He then tells you what the evidence of this new life looks like. "But the fruit of the Spirit is love, joy, peace, forbearance, kindness, goodness, faithfulness, gentleness and self-control. Against such things there is no law" (Galatians 5:22–23).
>
> "Do not get drunk on wine, which leads to debauchery. Instead, be filled with the Spirit" (Ephesians 5:18).
>
> This word for filled is *pleroo*: *Strong's* G4137. It means filled inwardly or made complete, to influence fully.

Whenever you see this word *pleroo* (filling) attached to a person, it is tied to the nature of God, which is the sign of new birth.

- "And to know this love that surpasses knowledge—that you may be filled to the measure of all the fullness of God" (Ephesians 3:19).
- "Filled with the fruit of righteousness that comes through Jesus Christ—to the glory and praise of God" (Philippians 1:11).

The evidence of the *pleroo* filling of the Spirit is the fruit of the Spirit, which represents the character or nature of God. We are restored back to the image of God, and now we can continue God's first command to multiply his image.

The second work of the Holy Spirit is to empower us to fulfill our divine purpose.

There is a second Greek word for filled, *pletho*: *Strong's* 4130. It means to furnish, accomplish, fill, supply.

We see this filling on the day of Pentecost. "All of them were filled with the Holy Spirit and began to speak in other tongues as the Spirit enabled them" (Acts 2:4).

What was the purpose for this filling? To furnish or supply them with power to continue to carry on the mission of Jesus.

How was the power expressed? Through the gifts of the Spirit.

The church expanded immediately after the disciples were pletho-filled, not because of sound preaching. It was the powerful demonstration of the gifts of the Spirit of God that revealed something miraculous had happened. The people were in awe and ready to hear and respond to the message.

Notice the difference when people are pletho-filled.

John the Baptist was pletho-filled to carry on the work of a prophet. "For he will be great in the sight of the Lord. He is never to take wine or other fermented drink, and he will be filled with the Holy Spirit even before he is born" (Luke 1:15).

Elizabeth was pletho-filled and prophesied to Mary. "When Elizabeth heard Mary's greeting, the baby leaped in her womb, and Elizabeth was filled with the Holy Spirit" (Luke 1:41).

Zechariah was pletho-filled and also prophesied. "His father Zechariah was filled with the Holy Spirit and prophesied" (Luke 1:67).

Peter was pletho-filled and made a bold proclamation about the works of Jesus. Acts 4:8–10 states:

> Then Peter, filled with the Holy Spirit, said to them: "Rulers and elders of the people! If we are being called to account today for an act of kindness shown to a man who was lame and are being asked how he was healed, then know this, you and all the people of Israel: It is by the name of Jesus Christ of Nazareth, whom you crucified but whom God raised from the dead, that this man stands before you healed."

The early church prayed for a pletho filling and described what it would look like. Healing, signs, and wonders, and boldness—all evidences of the gifts of the Spirit. "Now, Lord, consider their threats and enable your servants to speak your word with great boldness. Stretch out your hand to heal and perform signs and wonders through the name of your holy servant Jesus" (Acts 4:29–30).

After Saul's conversion (pleroo filling) on the Damascus road, he was pletho-filled, when Ananias laid hands on him, and he became the apostle Paul and was used mightily to expand the kingdom of God. "Then Ananias went to the house and entered it. Placing his hands on Saul, he said, 'Brother Saul, the Lord—Jesus, who appeared to you on the road as you were coming here—has sent me so that you may see again and be filled with the Holy Spirit'" (Acts 9:17).

When Jesus was about to ascend, he told the disciples to wait for the promise of the Father. The promise here was to restore our divine purpose to reign as his divine partners. "I am going to send you what my Father has promised; but stay in the city until you have been clothed with power from on high" (Luke 24:49).

So what was the point of this said power? "But you will receive power when the Holy Spirit comes on you; and you will be my witnesses in Jerusalem, and in all Judea and Samaria, and to the ends of the earth" (Acts 1:8).

To continue the work that Jesus started, which was preaching and demonstrating the kingdom so that the earth would look like heaven. "Jesus replied, 'While you were ministering, I watched Satan topple until he fell suddenly from heaven like lightning to the ground. Now you understand that I have imparted to you all my authority to trample over his kingdom. You will trample upon every demon before you and overcome every power Satan possesses. Absolutely nothing will be able to harm you as you walk in this authority'" (Luke 10:18–19).

A man of the Word and the Spirit is pursuing the heart of God. He lives out of the overflow of being in the presence of and moves in the power and love of God to reveal the will of God so that the earth would look like heaven. Wholeness, fullness, joy, peace, unity, and equality, just to name a few—how cool would that be?

Satan's strategy

Convince the church that there is no need for the supernatural, taking away the very witness that God intended to draw people to himself.

CHAPTER 11

I Am a Son

It is impossible to properly interpret
scripture apart from relationship.

—Jim Nave

YOU WERE CREATED for relationship! To fully understand sonship, I want to remind you of an early revelation: "All of God's plans flow from his nature, and all of his promises are backed by his nature."

Mankind was created out of God's nature of infinite love. Some might think that he is a narcissist looking for love and approval, so he made man to love and worship him. That cannot be further from the truth. He made mankind because he needed a way of expressing his infinite love.

We are the objects of his affection. He made us because he is a relational being. We have to understand that Adam and Eve had a real relationship with God, and we can imagine that included some of the relational components as any other family dynamic. It was a three-way dialogue, they told stories, shared their hopes and dreams, laughed until they cried, all of the things included in a healthy relationship. It was awesome and amazing, just the way God designed it.

The enemy knew about the power of intimacy. He experienced it in heaven before his rebellion. If he could no longer experience the infinite love of God, he would make sure that no one else would either. So he devised and implemented a plan that would separate God from his children.

There must have been a great celebration in the dark atmosphere of the enemy when Jesus breathed his last breath on the cross. Can't you just hear the little demons congratulating their boss on a job well done?

On the third day, when Jesus rose again, the atmosphere changed from darkness to a brilliant white as Jesus defeated the enemy once and for all. It must have been a very chaotic scene as they went from victory to defeat in an instant.

Suddenly, the enemy took the stage and calmed his crowd of demons. He might have said something like, "We might have lost the battle, but we can still win the war. I will use my power of deception to twist God's message, just enough so they can have a confession of redemption with no expression of it. Then we can keep them under our influence and keep them from influencing future generations. Here is what I will do, I will

- get them to focus on a future hope, telling them that when Jesus returns or they die, then they will be made whole and the relationship will be restored;
- create a gospel that is self-centered in nature. They will come to God to get their needs met, and it will continue to feed the selfish nature I gave them. On Sundays, they will sing it is all about him, but they will prove by their lives that it is still all about them;
- get them to interpret the Scriptures through human reason and intellect, causing them to reject anything they can't understand, removing the power of the Gospel to restore them back to wholeness and fullness, thus causing people to question the goodness of God;
- I will get them to focus on knowing about God so they will spend all their time studying about him and never develop an intimate relationship with him, causing them to miss out on the promise of abiding fruit. I will convince them that God only speaks through the written Word so they will never make time to hear the most intimate, affectionate, personal words he has for them. I will cause them to

emphasize orthodoxy apart from relationship, so instead of expressing the love of God, they will talk about the judgment of God, causing great separation and destruction as people move apart from the heart of God;

- most importantly, I will put a veil over their spiritual eyes that will allow them to read and hear that they are sons and daughters, yet still live like orphans so that

    - they will never enter into the secret place where the Father waits for them with delight and joyful expectation;
    - they will have no concept of experiencing the warmth of the Father's touch;
    - they will never hear the whisper of the Father's affirming voice;
    - they won't understand the Father's covenant of favor with expectations of goodness;
    - they will never experience the pleasure of the Father as he reminds them that they were chosen as his heir before the foundation of the world;
    - they will never be hidden under the shadow of his wings while the enemy passes by;
    - they will never cling to the rock of their salvation while the whole earth is in shambles;
    - they will never feel the tender touch of God's correction;
    - they will never feel the unconditional love of restoration after a momentary failure and repentance;
    - they will never experience the promise to bear fruit as the Father flows through them with his power and love."

I want to share a parable that I believe is straight from the heart of God for you! Before you read it, I want you to take a few minutes, just to thank God that everything that the enemy has caused you to believe about you is a lie. Take a moment to renounce any lies that you have believed. Now begin to thank God for his goodness toward you, thank him that he came to set you free from the power and influence of the enemy and restore you back to your original image and purpose. When you begin to feel hope and peace rise up, thank him once again and continue reading.

I am who God says I am!

Let's first start with what God says about you.
Romans 8:14–17 states:

> For those who are led by the Spirit of God are the children of God. The Spirit you received does not make you slaves, so that you live in fear again; rather, the Spirit you received brought about your adoption to sonship. And by him we cry, "Abba, Father." The Spirit himself testifies with our spirit that we are God's children. Now if we are children, then we are heirs—heirs of God and co-heirs with Christ, if indeed we share in his sufferings in order that we may also share in his glory.

Now let's read the parable.

Little Johnny was an orphan. When he was nine years old, both of his parents died in a tragic car accident. No other family members were willing to take care of him, so he ended up in an orphanage. It was a dark place. The adults were verbally abusive. They would say things like maybe your parents didn't really die, they were just embarrassed by you and wanted to start over. They constantly reminded him that he was an orphan and he would always be one. Out of frustration, they would call him a loser and say he would never amount to anything; he is just a dirty orphan. One night, after his nightly prayers, he fell asleep and had a dream. In his dream, a man who looked a lot like the picture of Jesus that was on the wall in the hallway came with adoption papers. This man helped him pack his meager belongings and whisked him off, put him in a car, and said he was taking him to meet his Father. He slept for what seemed like an eternity.

Finally, the man woke him up, and the first thing that Johnny saw was a sign that said "Welcome to the kingdom." The man grabbed the boy's hand and said, "Come with me. We are home." The man took Johnny into the most beautiful castle he had ever seen. He asked for a tour, but the man said that there was something that must be done before he could really enjoy the castle.

The man led Johnny down a large corridor and opened the last door on the right. Inside was a giant tub. The man turned on the water, undressed the boy, closely examining his dirty, bruised body. After the tub was full, he placed the boy in it. Then the man removed his outer garments and exposed the scars in his hands and side. He began to sing the most beautiful song to Johnny. His voice was majestic, like nothing he had ever heard before. The boy was so overwhelmed with love that he could not even make out the words, but it didn't matter.

For the first time in his life, he knew what unconditional love and acceptance felt like. Then the man put his hand in his side and pulled out what appeared to be a fragrant balm. First he rubbed it on his external wounds, bringing healing to the places caused by the nipping and biting of other orphans. Then he placed the healing balm on his head. Suddenly, the boy could feel fear, worry, anxiety, and every form of negativity melt away. Lastly, he took the balm and placed it on his heart. He felt, hatred, unforgiveness, and judgment melt away, and his heart was filled with a love he never knew was possible.

Suddenly, he had a vision of the adults from the orphanage, but instead of his normal feelings of hatred, a great sense of compassion rose up in him, and he knew what it meant to finally be free.

The man dried him off and dressed him in a set of perfectly white clothes. The boy asked about the significance of the white clothes, and he said, "You have been washed as white as snow. From this point forward, we will remember your sins no more. Everything you have ever done or had done to you has been paid for and forgotten. We will never look back, and neither should you. You are no longer an orphan. You are a son, perfect in every way."

Next the young man leads him down another corridor and through the largest doors he has ever seen. He was breathless upon entering this room. It was like entering into another atmosphere. There was what appeared to be fog, but instead of it being scary, it was inviting. As they continued to walk through the fog, he began to hear melodious voices singing, "Holy, holy, holy is the Lord God Almighty." Then he began to see images floating around that appeared to be angels. Suddenly, the fog began to clear, and he realized he was standing in front of a giant golden throne that was covered with jewels. Then he heard a voice say, "Welcome." When he looked up, he saw what appeared to be a man, but his countenance was as bright as the sun, his eyes were like fire, and his voice was like a thousand melodies and harmonies all at the same time.

The boy fell on his face before him. There was a sense of fear or reverence, but he also felt completely drawn to him. Suddenly, without even trying, a song came out of his mouth, and he also was singing, "Holy, holy, holy is the Lord God Almighty."

Without warning, the Father grabbed the boy's hand and pulled him onto his lap. He said, "Before the foundation of the world, I chose you to be my son. In spite of everything you did or what was done to you, I never lost sight of your value. I looked through time and eternity and said, 'That is my boy, and doesn't he look just like me?' I have always delighted in you, waiting for the day when you would call out for me. Even in the darkest times, my thoughts were always with you, more than the sands of every shore, I couldn't wait to tell you about all the plans I have for you, plans for a hope and a future. I have always known your thoughts, and now you can know my thoughts, too, so we can get back to what I always dreamed of, an intimate relationship with you."

The Father grabbed the boy's hand and said, "You are not just my son but also my coheir, just like my other Son. Let's walk. I want to show you some of your inheritance, at least as much as you can handle for today. My treasures are endless, and you will spend a glorious lifetime receiving them and using them to bless other people."

The castle appeared to have endless corridors with doors on both sides, stretching out as far as the eyes could see. The Father said, "Inside each door is just one individual gift, and all of them together make up my total inheritance." He told the boy that there was nothing he could do to earn them. They are free. His only part is to believe and receive.

They entered into one corridor, and the Father said, "Let's start here." The rooms of the corridor were vast, and they were all plainly marked. One said love. As the boy opened the door, he began to get a glimpse of the enormity of his inheritance. In that vast room was enough love for everyone in the whole kingdom. The next door was joy, then peace, patience, kindness, goodness, gentleness, faithfulness, and self-control. They entered into another corridor, only these rooms were marked wisdom, revelation, power, authority, favor, blessing, treasure. The doors seem to go on and on, and there seemed to be no end to the provision of this benevolent King. The Father said, "My treasures are endless, and you will spend a glorious lifetime receiving them and using them to bless other people."

After the amazing tour, the Father headed to the top of the castle where they could see his entire kingdom. He asked Johnny if he could see what he sees. It was like Johnny could see the whole world at the same time. Every nation on earth was gathered under their national flag, every tribe and tongue, red, brown, yellow, black, and white, then he said they really are all precious in his sight. With his voice trembling with compassion, he said, "Every one of them is worth the blood of my Son and made for my image."

Then He told his son that he himself never leaves the castle, so he was sending Johnny to the earth to be his divine partner there. He told his son he would be with him and partner with him so that everyone on the earth would experience what he had just experienced. The son looked confused and asked him, "How can you stay here and be with me at the same time?"

The Father said, "Son, that is a great question. I have someone else I would like to introduce you to. He is the third member of my family. He is the Holy Spirit. The three of us all work together—Father, Son, and Holy Spirit. I am the Creator, my son is the Redeemer, and the Holy Spirit is our divine partner on the earth. He will not just go with you. He will live inside of you. I will work through him, just as if I were there with you. He will be the conduit through which all of my inheritance will flow. I will work through you just like I did through Abraham, Moses, Joshua, Peter, Paul and, yes, even Jesus. My design is to do the same things through you that I did through them. I know this sounds crazy, but my work will not diminish but increase. I will do greater things through you if you believe!" His last words to his son were, "With man, this is impossible, but with God, all things are possible."

When Johnny woke up from the dream, he was still in the orphanage, but he knew in his heart he was no longer an orphan but a son of the Most High God.

For many of you, this sounds too good to be true, too far-fetched. For some, maybe even heresy. It's time we stop believing the deception of the enemy. We have to stop settling for anything less than the whole truth. Then and only then can we start walking in our true God-given identity and impact the earth with the goodness of God.

I want to finish this book with one of my favorite quotes.

> It would seem that Our Lord finds our desires not too strong, but too weak. We are half-hearted creatures, fooling about with drink and sex and ambition when infinite joy is offered us, like an ignorant child who wants to go on making mud pies in a slum because he cannot imagine what is meant by the offer of a holiday at the sea. We are far too easily pleased.
>
> —C. S. Lewis

Please receive this prayer:

Father, I pray that your child would get a revelation of who you truly are, the immensity of your love for them, and the price that you paid so that they can have an intimate relationship with you and be restored back to your image and likeness and bring glory to you by revealing your true nature to the world. Amen.

ABOUT THE AUTHOR

Jim Nave is a passionate follower of Jesus Christ, a minister, and Bible teacher. He is also the founder and president of Reveal Him Ministries, a global ministry which is committed to revealing the goodness of God to the world. He has been married to his wife, Teresa, for forty years, has five children and fifteen grandchildren. He has an AA degree in biblical studies and a BA degree in theology from Andersonville Theological Seminary.

To contact Pastor Jim or schedule a speaking engagement, you can reach him at revealhim.life.